How University Boards Work

How University Boards Work

*A Guide for Trustees, Officers, and Leaders
in Higher Education*

Robert A. Scott

Johns Hopkins University Press · *Baltimore*

© 2018 Johns Hopkins University Press
All rights reserved. Published 2018
Printed in the United States of America on acid-free paper
9 8 7 6 5 4 3 2

Johns Hopkins University Press
2715 North Charles Street
Baltimore, Maryland 21218-4363
www.press.jhu.edu

Library of Congress Cataloging-in-Publication Data

Names: Scott, Robert A. (Robert Allyn), 1939- author.
Title: How university boards work : a guide for trustees, officers, and leaders
    in higher education / Robert A. Scott.
Description: Baltimore : Johns Hopkins University Press, 2018. |
    Includes bibliographical references and index.
Identifiers: LCCN 2017033310 | ISBN 9781421424941 (pbk. : alk. paper) |
    ISBN 1421424940 (pbk. : alk. paper) | ISBN 9781421424958 (electronic) |
    ISBN 1421424959 (electronic)
Subjects: LCSH: College trustees—United States—Handbooks, manuals, etc. |
    College administrators—United States—Handbooks, manuals, etc. |
    Universities and colleges—United States—Administration—Handbooks,
    manuals, etc.
Classification: LCC LB2342.5 .S36 2018 | DDC 378.1/011—dc23
LC record available at https://lccn.loc.gov/2017033310

A catalog record for this book is available from the British Library.

*Special discounts are available for bulk purchases of this book. For more information,
please contact Special Sales at 410-516-6936 or specialsales@press.jhu.edu.*

Johns Hopkins University Press uses environmentally friendly book materials,
including recycled text paper that is composed of at least 30 percent post-
consumer waste, whenever possible.

Contents

Preface

During my thirty years as a college president—fifteen years at Adelphi University and fifteen years at Ramapo College—I served with many trustees. Counting my higher education service, nonprofit organization board membership, and company board involvement, I estimate that I have served with more than 400 board members. Many are memorable. While I recount the contributions of those who were especially helpful and characterize those who were not, I do not mention names. This guide for higher education trustees and others responsible for governing and leading institutions of higher education, whether privately financed or state funded, is written from personal experience and considerable research. I started this reflection on university governance and leadership by asking a question:

How did we get here?

In other words, how did we arrive at the forms of university governance now in use? And how can we govern most effectively given our understanding of past and current trends in higher education?

I was at the University of Oxford when I asked this question. Since this venerable institution was the source for the governance pattern at Harvard University, the first higher education institution in the United States, I asked people I knew there and those they recommended to guide me to sources about governance. David Palfreyman of New College, Oxford, and Michael Shattock, formerly of the University of Warwick and now a visiting professor at University College London Institute of

Education, have written about university governance with elegance and insight, and each directed me to helpful resources.

Books and Articles of Interest

The books and articles I read or referenced while preparing this guide to governance were of varying quality and utility. Some were superficial, others too theoretical. The most insightful and helpful for my consideration of university governance and leadership were books by William (Bill) Bowen, Dick Chait, David Palfreyman, and Michael Shattock, as well as articles by Dick Chait, Darryl Greer, and David Nadler. Each often wrote with coauthors or coeditors of considerable repute. Helpful articles and reports were most often those published by the Association of Governing Boards of Universities and Colleges (AGB), the Organisation for Economic Co-operation and Development (OECD), and BoardMax, a Cleveland-based organization serving nonprofit and public sector agencies in meeting the needs of good board governance.

For my deeper understanding of university leadership, and leadership in general, I count books by James MacGregor Burns, Harlan Cleveland, Nannerl Keohane, John Lombardi, Elizabeth Samet, and Stephen Joel Trachtenberg and associates as among the most helpful.

For reportage on current events and contemporary themes in higher education, I find the *Chronicle of Higher Education, Inside Higher Ed*, and *Education Dive* to be the best at original writing and at aggregating the work of others. I read them every day. Fortunately, *The Atlantic, Harper's Magazine*, the *New York Times*, the *Wall Street Journal*, and the *Washington Post* also give attention to higher education issues, in varying degrees of detail. The organizations I found most helpful, and to which university trustees should turn for assistance, include the AGB and the American Council on Education (ACE).

Well-known events and developments in higher education do not all have corresponding citations in the text, as they are easily found in the relevant sources in the bibliography. References indicated in the text relate to issues, topics, events, and actions that are comparatively lesser known. In the following, I discuss references in three categories: board governance, presidential leadership, and books and articles that provide an overview of higher education history, policy, and contemporary challenges.

Board Governance

While many of the books and articles on boards are divorced from the complexities of university governance, there are some that are essential reading. Books by William Bowen, Clark Kerr, John Kirkpatrick, and Samuel Morison on the history and development of American university governing models help us understand how we got to where we are. On the same list of essential reading are articles by several authors writing for AGB's *Trusteeship* and other periodicals. These include William Bowen again, José Cabranes, Richard Chait, Darryl Greer, and David Nadler. They offer lessons from experience on how to conceptualize what works and why. Finally, I think it is important to read critiques of university governance and leadership. Among these, I include other works by AGB authors as well as works by Derek Bok, Brian Mitchell, and Thorsten Veblen, and select articles from *Inside Higher Ed*.

Presidential Leadership

There are many books and articles on leadership. While most are related to leadership in business, industry, and politics, there are some on university leadership, and a few of these are quite good. Some were written by retired presidents in an attempt to offer reflections on their careers. In other cases the authors use a case study approach, and in still others they use a more autobiographical approach to discuss how leadership is exercised.

Overall, I commend the Robert Adams translation of Machiavelli's *The Prince* and books by William Bowen, James Fisher and associates, Barbara Kellerman, Nannerl Keohane, John Lombardi, and Stephen Joel Trachtenberg and associates. These offer comprehensive analyses of leadership and how it can be exercised in universities.

Higher Education Overview

Governing board members should know the history not only of their institution but also of higher education at large, the evolution of public policies regarding higher education, and the pros and cons of contemporary issues affecting colleges and universities. Among the most helpful and readable books and articles on the higher education landscape are those by Derek Bok, Jonathan Cole, Andrew Delbanco, Christopher Jencks and David Riesman, Frederick Rudolf, and Laurence Veysey. In addition, *Inside Higher Ed* provides daily portraits of institutions and issues that are essential reading for any well-informed higher education leader.

Just as a corporate board member should know about the history and context of his or her company's purpose, market, and competitive advantage, so also should a university board member know about higher education's unique purposes and characteristics. Why was a college started? What government policies and programs have been critical to the development of individual institutions and higher education at large? What are current issues and pressures on universities that board members should understand? These and other questions are explored in the books and articles recommended here, especially in the articles from AGB and in Lawrence Gladieux's remarkable book on Congress and higher education.

In addition to reading, I interviewed board members and presidents about the pressures they experienced in governance and leadership, and sought their advice about issues and best practices. Those interviewed include the following:

These colleagues and friends shared their insights and experiences, and some commented on draft portions of the manuscript. I am grateful for their help, but do not hold them responsible for the results.

Bill Bowen famously said, "Board governance is a team sport." It is a team sport in the sense that the board must speak as one and is led by a captain and a coach. And, just as a team must work as a whole, so board members are part of a collective effort. Therefore, the orientation to and guidance for board service are ongoing. It should not stop with Orientation 101, but should be a continuing effort of the Trustee Affairs or Board Governance Committee. Continuing orientation should include briefings by university officers, consultants on special topics and facilitators at board retreats, and members of the audit and legal firms representing the institution; attendance at meetings of state and national associations; and reading—frequent reading. The books and articles listed in the bibliography and referenced throughout are all part of an ongoing orientation to effective board governance.

Acknowledgments

Writing a book is both a lonely journey and a group project. For this reason, I want to first thank Greg Britton, editorial director at Johns Hopkins University Press, and Stephen Joel Trachtenberg, president emeritus of George Washington University, for their encouragement and support. I also am grateful to the staff and consultants at Johns Hopkins University Press for their editorial assistance.

I started work on this project while on sabbatical from Adelphi University and serving as senior visiting research scholar at the Rothermere American Institute and visiting fellow at Mansfield College, University of Oxford, in fall 2015. I am obliged to Nigel Bowles and Jay Sexton at the Rothermere Institute for their support while there.

When I returned to New York City and resumed my sabbatical post as a Frederick Lewis Allen Room Scholar at the New York Public Library, I began my research in the library's magnificent holdings. Jean Strouse and Melanie Locay at the library were terrific in their support and assistance, and for that I am thankful.

As I continued my research, I developed lists of books and articles on university governance to read, scholars and practitioners to interview, and organizations to consult. Those interviewed for this book or in earlier years for other projects, and their titles, are listed in the preface. They are scholars, practitioners, and legal experts. I am grateful to them for sharing their insights, prompting my thinking, and introducing me to others and to references. I am particularly indebted to Vartan Gregorian, president of the Carnegie Corporation of New York, and the late Bill Bowen, then at Ithaka in Princeton.

There are several trustees with whom I served that I would like to mention by name. Each is referenced anonymously in the text, but they were so helpful to my development that I want to acknowledge them directly. Millicent Anisfield, Theodore R. Lilley, and Robert Corman were trustees of Ramapo College of New Jersey, and Jack Bierwirth, Steve Fischer, Joan Girgus, Leon Pollack, and Philip Winterer were trustees at Adelphi University. I learned a great deal from each of them. I admire them and am grateful for their contributions to my education as a college president, as a board member, and as a person.

I also want to thank my children, Ryan and Kira, and my stepchildren, Kate and Chris, for their forbearance in knowing that this book project meant so much to me even as it intruded on family time.

Finally, but not least, I want to thank my wife, Carole Artigiani, founder of Global Kids, Inc., a remarkable youth development organization now in its twenty-ninth year. She created an unusual and effective board organization at the beginning and was a wise counselor during my eighteen months of talking incessantly about governance and leadership. She also is a skilled reader and editor who helped me in the final preparation of the manuscript. However, any errors or inelegant phrasing are entirely my own.

How University Boards Work

Why a Guide?

Higher education is one of America's most cherished assets. Families celebrate the twenty-two-year-old and the older adult upon graduation. The public values higher education for its part in social and economic advancement, scientific discoveries, and cultural contributions, and says that college is worth the cost in terms of individual and public benefit. Yet many in our society are also increasingly "mistrustful of college costs, leadership and value."[1] How can these two attitudes exist side by side? The answer seems to be that while a college education is highly valued, there is significant debate regarding the ideal management of our institutions of higher education.

Those most responsible for higher education's educational and business practices are college and university presidents and boards of trustees. Who are these trustees? How are they selected? How are they prepared for their duties? To whom are they accountable? This book aims to illuminate these questions and to guide campus presidents and boards in effective leadership of their institutions.

Leaders in higher education are challenged by a broad range of political, economic, organizational, technological, historical, and social dynamics. Political and economic issues confronting the president and the board include declining public funding and alumni giving, criticisms of increasing tuition rates, inadequate career services, reductions in state and federal financial aid, student and institutional debt, loan default and graduation rates, budget constraints that result in inadequate salary increases for faculty and staff, emphasis on career education over liberal arts and sciences curricula, and pressure to spend more institutional endowment income in order to reduce tuition rates. At the same time, there are pressures to improve campus productivity and to meet new and elevated federal compliance requirements and regional accrediting body expectations and standards. The president and board need to make a range of economic decisions affecting everything from academic quality, to the purchase of new property, to concerns about the commercialization of campus research.

Universities and colleges must respond to the challenges of increased and intensified competition from neighboring institutions. They must balance rising tuition and increased operational costs with the need to discount tuition in order to provide both need- and merit-based financial aid to qualified incoming students. The board and the president have multiple targets for growth, whether in the number of applicants, the number of students on campus, the amount of net tuition income, the size of endowed funds, the rates of graduation, and even the competitiveness of sports teams. Additionally, technological advances and the changing demographics of students require decisions to be made about whether or how much to invest in new technologies for online and distance education as well as for science and medical laboratories.

Institutions should not be aloof from society, ivory towers set apart. Universities and colleges must maintain and build relationships with a wide variety of institutional constituents, each with a different agenda. These relationships require consideration of gubernatorial and legislative interference; faculty and graduate student unionization; job placement rates for graduates; student activism on a range of social, political, and economic issues; diversity in student admissions, faculty and staff hiring, and board membership; and even admissions priorities for athletes, veterans, or the children and grandchildren of alumni. There are decisions to be made about faculty personnel and the institutional reward system to balance teaching, advising, and research publications. Many partnerships necessary for off-campus opportunities, such as clinical placements or internships, require involvement of the university in the broader community.

The president, board, staff, faculty, students, alumni, and state and federal agencies must respect a system of shared governance, which is necessary in order to balance the needs of all parties involved while staying true to the historical mission and values of the institution. University boards are sometimes criticized for doing too little in guiding their institutions and at other times criticized for intruding too much into the province of management. This can be a tricky balance to maintain.

The challenges trustees face are in many ways more daunting than ever, as perceptions of higher education institutions as moribund and expensive become pervasive. To protect the institution, it is important to remind politicians and others who control college and university funding and policy that a larger portion of the population than ever is involved in higher education. Colleges and universities are anchors for community and economic development. In addition to preparing a highly educated work force as well as engaged citizens, institutions of higher education generate payroll and other taxes and employ more than 4 million people, of whom 1.5 million are faculty. Total revenues for higher education are over $500 billion, with endowments totaling more than $500 billion.[2] They also provide significant cultural contributions, including music, theater, dance, painting, sculpture, athletics, and children's programs. Some colleges have nursery schools, and over the years many have developed K-12 lab schools to develop and improve our educational system. Strong, effective, and moral leaders and trustees are needed to serve as a voice representing the enduring values of higher education.

The Business Model of Higher Education

One criticism about higher education that generally comes from within is that institutions are becoming too "corporate." It is alleged that they have forgotten the purposes and values that have distinguished higher learning and continue to do so.

The business or economic model of higher education is also criticized as "broken" by public officials and media pundits. These complaints usually allege the following: annual tuition increases with too little attention paid to controlling costs; slow pace of change from lectures to massive open online courses (MOOCs) or the adoption of other new technology to improve access to instruction and lower its costs; resistance to addressing public needs; increasing student debt; new programs and services added without eliminating any so as to use resources more efficiently; and too much construction of new buildings, some of which are perceived to be frills (such as the assertion that libraries are no longer essential due to the increased accessibility of online information and instruction).

In response, defenders of higher education complain about the encroachment of corporate models of governance and assessment on academic institutions, and point to the damaging effects of reductions in state funding, often as a consequence of tax cuts, as a leading cause of lower graduation rates and increases in tuition. They also refer to the increased focus on job training as an institutional mission, as well as a mandate to use part-time or contingent faculty instead of full-time faculty in order to reduce labor costs while increasing the size of the administrative staff in order to strengthen management controls.

These criticisms contain some truth. Technology holds great promise for enhancing teaching and learning, and most institutions have the technological platform necessary to support distance education, even if that platform is not sufficient for MOOCs with tens of thousands of students. Policies and practices must be in place for students who want to transfer in credit from online courses taken at other colleges or in high school, athletes and debate team members who need to touch base with their classes, submit papers, and receive feedback while off campus, and faculty who are attending conferences but need to stay in contact with their students. In addition, many alumni work in fields that require continuing professional education and would like to complete that work at their alma mater. For all these reasons, universities should support the basic infrastructure for distance learning.

The charge of corporatization in university governance is related to perceptions that universities are focused on short-term instead of long-term thinking; the market more than the university's mission; abandoning shared governance; eroding autonomy in academic research and professional priorities; considering faculty as "producers" and students as "consumers"; silencing voices of dissent; giving higher priority to the marketing of activities than to improving program quality; adopting the belief that teaching and learning can benefit from certain productivity measures that are not appropriate for education; and giving more attention to financial returns than to improving student and faculty success.

One sign of corporatization is in the increasing number of part-time and contingent faculty. They cost less to employ than full-time faculty. In fact, some colleges teach nearly 70 percent of course sections with part-time faculty.[3] But part-time faculty members are not as available for advising students, sponsoring student clubs, developing curriculum, managing internships, nurturing younger faculty, and serving on faculty and university-wide committees.

The lament about adjunct faculty is not to deny the value of employing some part-time faculty whose expertise would be too expensive or is not in sufficient demand to justify hiring them on a full-time basis, but is desirable to include as a supplement to the curriculum. Nor is this to say that universities must ignore the financial bottom line. Of course universities must balance their budgets and even have a surplus. Universities must use human, capital, and financial resources efficiently and effectively. Waste is waste, in any enterprise.

This outsourcing of student instruction is similar to other forms of outsourcing in society. It gives higher priority to profit margins than to mission and quality assurance, and it is part of a trend to employ an increasing number of for-profit companies to provide services that at one time were the province of faculty members. These services include course management systems, student success services, and tools for monitoring student progress.

Another set of complaints is about the apparent erosion of intellectual values in favor of market and managerial values, resulting in the sapping of the soul of an institution as it becomes a joyless but glossy shell of its former self, losing sight of its mission. There is a legitimate role for university research into questions of climate change, evolution, and financial misdeeds, among other topics. To shy away from these and similar topics because some people call them controversial is to adopt a corporate view. Universities should be focused on transformations, in terms of knowledge, skills, abilities, and values, not on transactions for profit alone.

Unlike corporations, where there is generally one bottom line, universities have multiple bottom lines. The academic president's role is different from that of the corporate chief because of the former's commitment to a mission and a heritage. The corporate chief's obligation is to the bottom line and to shareholders' financial interests. If a product or service is no longer competitive, there is little constraint in eliminating it. We all know of companies that have dramatically changed the business they are in over a relatively short period of time. A company's mission can be changed from accounting and auditing to consulting and advising, or from manufacturing hardware to providing software and processing, in relatively rapid order.

The scholar, university president, and foundation executive Bill Bowen said, "While a for-profit board has an obligation to get out of a bad business, a non-profit board (including university boards) may have an obligation to stay in an activity if it is to be true to its mission."[4] Academic institutions cannot change their missions so quickly. They have a state charter that specifies the mission and are regulated by the state and federal governments. Yes, they need to change program mix and degree offerings in response to societal needs, and they do so. But these changes must be approved by the state because these institutions are tax-exempt organizations and operate under a set of laws designed to protect the public and the charitable donations of those who support the institution.

Unlike the goals of a corporation or private business, with profit, market share, and, for some, share price, of primary importance, the goals for an institution of higher education can be elusive. When the goals are prestige or moving up in national or regional rankings, the strategies are not always clear. Even for more fundamental goals, such as increasing the graduation rate or improving placements of graduating seniors in graduate and professional schools, the means of achieving an institution's objectives are complex and multifaceted.

The Benefits of a Guide

The following inventory of concerns about college and university governance and leadership is based on my experience as well as on the results of interviews of trustees and campus presidents for this book. These elements of the higher education model concern me the most, and I have grouped them according to the party most responsible for making changes and improvements. This guide will explore approaches to address the concerns.

Trustees

The following concerns can be addressed through guide books and orientation programs as well as the publications and meetings of the Association of Governing Boards of Universities and Colleges (AGB):

- Boards that know little about the enterprise of higher education, often due to inadequate orientation programs for trustees, unlike the boards of corporations, which more often than not want members who are knowledgeable about a company's purpose for being, its business model, and the industry in which it competes
- Trustees who are ignorant of higher education's capacity to respond to forces of change and societal imperatives, as shown by the history of colleges and universities
- Trustees who do not understand how general measures of productivity in the private sector may not obtain the same results in the university setting (for example, hiring more part-time instead of full-time faculty may reduce the cost of instruction but lead to lower student completion rates)
- Trustees who are apt to offer prescriptions or recommendations before asking questions about the greater purpose behind how or why organizational decisions are made
- Trustees who neither understand the need for academic freedom nor respect the four essential freedoms of higher education
- Board chairs who act in an imperial manner and do not ensure that all voices are heard

Presidents

The following concerns can be addressed by guidance from the board and by attendance at professional meetings and programs, such as those offered by Harvard University for new and continuing presidents:

- Campus presidents who serve as a corporate-style chief executive officer (CEO), focusing on finance and external relations, rather than as chief education officer focused on the purposes of higher education and the enhancement of opportunities for teaching and learning, resulting in alienation from the faculty, the heart of the institution, as one consequence
- Campus presidents who delegate leadership of the faculty to someone else, instead of chairing meetings of the faculty where the critical issues of purpose, curriculum, standards, student needs, values, and the socialization of new faculty can be put center stage
- Campus presidents who have only limited or no experience outside academe and therefore are limited in their vision of possibilities
- Campus presidents who place more emphasis on the board as a source of philanthropy than as partners in governance and strategy
- Campus presidents who view trustees as the enemy rather than as partners in governing
- Campus presidents who pay more attention to the characteristics of the institution's aspirational peers than to those of realistic models to emulate, including those that are catching up
- Campus presidents who reduce budgets by employing more contingent and part-time faculty instead of engaging in a serious study of the cost structure and taking necessary and appropriate actions
- Campus presidents who respond to reductions in revenues by making across-the-board cuts to budgets, instead of taking a more strategic approach
- Campus presidents who advocate tuition discounting and institutional financial aid distributions that are designed more to reward students who will help raise the campus academic profile for a college-guide ranking than to help

make the campus more affordable for talented students from low-income families
- Campus presidents who adopt new technologies without a plan for their most effective and efficient uses in teaching, learning, and processing information

Trustees and Presidents

The following concerns regarding the partnership between trustees and presidents require thoughtful consideration and often benefit from the help of consultants:

- Leaders who sponsor a reward system that ties the faculty closer to their disciplines and a graduate-school model of teaching and research rather than to the satisfaction, success, retention, and graduation goals of the institution and its undergraduate students
- Leaders who "reward" faculty by releasing them from teaching and advising, which should be the major functions of the university
- Leaders who delegate student academic advising to staff members (who are undoubtedly talented and sincere in their work), when student advising should be an essential component of the faculty's teaching responsibility
- Leaders whose press for enrollment leads to ignoring the relationship between admissions criteria, academic expectations, and the learning environment, especially with regard to students with special needs, students on the autism spectrum, students from other countries whose English language preparation is inadequate, and other students who are admitted but not provided with sufficient assistance to be successful
- Leaders who seek to emulate doctoral research universities and blindly follow the serpentine path of mission creep, described by Riesman and Jencks in *The Academic Revolution*[5] as an undulating procession of institutions fol-

lowing the head of Harvard, even when groundbreaking research is not the likely outcome of changes in the mission statement or the teaching obligations of faculty

- Leaders who ignore the typologies of faculty scholarship, research, and other creative activity (Discovery, Integration, Application, and Teaching) as articulated by Ernest L. Boyer in *Scholarship Reconsidered*[6] when formulating the mission statement, goals for student learning, and expectations for faculty appointments, reappointments, tenure, promotion, and other rewards
- Leaders who focus on short-term goals and results instead of on long-term impact (e.g., emphasizing transactional means such as staff costs over transformational ends such as the role of faculty and staff in helping meet goals for student retention and graduation)
- Leaders who ignore the fact that dashboards, benchmarking, and related tools cannot prohibit failure but can lead to a false sense of security
- Leaders who consistently increase tuition without connecting tuition revenue to student learning outcomes
- Leaders who allocate increasing amounts of money to big-time athletics and advertising in ways that distort the academic values of the institution and whose results cannot be measured

Faculty

The following concerns can be addressed through strong, positive relations between and among trustees, presidents, chief academic officers, deans, and faculty leaders:

- Faculty whose only preparation to teach is their own experience as students, are not oriented to the institution's standards for excellence, and either ignore or are not offered professional development opportunities to improve their teaching

- Faculty who ignore their role as tutors and advisors of students and instead emphasize their role as "professors" of a discipline, doing their "own" work
- Faculty who advocate for the concept of shared governance but are not available for one-quarter of the year and are unwilling to identify and shed low-priority programs and activities
- Faculty who adopt general education programs that ignore the fact that a large percentage of students transfer in from other institutions

In light of these many challenges, boards and presidents need a tool for orienting board members to their duties and developing the valuable leadership required for guidance and management of institutions of higher education. It is damaging to an institution when a president resigns, retires early, or is forced out due to failed leadership. Presidential turnover can affect school morale and can end up costing millions of dollars. Boards have brought unwanted attention to themselves by hiring presidents whose claim to expertise is in business, politics, or the media, instead of academia, and by firing presidents within the first few months of their appointment. The reasons for turnover include a lack of clarity of expectations, dysfunctional boards, erratic or unethical behavior, political interference, student and faculty protests, and more. In some cases, the termination or resignation of the president occurs when the board and the president do not share common expectations for their respective roles. This has been true at elite research universities, regional public and independent institutions, historically black colleges, and community colleges around the country.

The challenges of effective management in the face of social, political, and economic changes are exacerbated by the twenty-four-hour, seven-days-a-week news cycle and the ubiquity of social media. Cases of racial and sexual assaults, bullying, suicides, school shootings, student deaths from excessive drinking, and other incidents can rapidly become publicized, thus creating pressures that distract leaders from the central issue that needs to be addressed.

Many trustees may think they do not need a guide to assist them in their service. Because of their experiences in business or on other boards, they think there is nothing more to learn about service on a university board. Unfortunately, this is not always the case. Some college and university board members know little more about higher education than what they remember from their days as students, what their children may have experienced, what they may have garnered when being asked for donations, or what they read or hear in news media. There are examples of board members who violate their duties by missing meetings, being unprepared for the agenda, or remaining silent; supporting a decision that favors an interested party and not the institution as a whole; failing to honor confidentiality; or ignoring the campus mission, charter, and core values in favor of some questionable initiative. Sometimes trustees at public institutions are unresponsive to campus constituents because they are politically appointed. Trustees need orientation, continuing professional development, and a handy guide for reference when making difficult discussions. As management consultant Peter Drucker once said,

> Both the businessman and the civil servant tend to underrate the difficulty of managing service institutions. The businessman thinks it is all a matter of being efficient; the civil servant thinks it is all a matter of having the right procedures and control. Both are wrong—service institutions [such as universities] are more complex than either businesses or government agencies—as we are painfully finding out in our attempts to make the hospital [or university] a little more manageable.[7]

This guide is intended to help clarify the role of trustees and overcome Drucker's assessment. Campus leaders must be reminded to stay true to the essence of higher education and remain committed to long-term, mission-based aspirations, rather than short-term, market-driven goals. The challenges of accountability, liability, and credibility all rest on the shoulders of trustees, no matter what type of institution they serve. The chapters to follow will provide an overview of the history and mission of institutions of higher education, review the responsibilities of the board and other campus leadership, outline the process of board membership, and recommend effective processes and procedures for the complex system of shared governance required at institutions of higher education.

The chapters in this book address the following questions:

- What are the distinctive features of governing in higher education?
- How are the boards of colleges and universities different from those in business and in other tax-exempt or non-profit organizations in terms of charter and responsibilities? In what ways are they similar?
- What is the art and craft of trusteeship?
- How are trustees prepared for their duties?
- What are the most significant challenges to being an effective trustee?
- What are effective ways of organizing the board's agendas in order to maximize discussion, understanding of the consequences of decisions, and board member satisfaction?
- What are the most important personnel responsibilities of board members?
- What are the characteristics of effective board-president relations?
- What forces are likely to have the greatest influence on the future of institutions of higher education?

I hope that this guide will assist boards in becoming more effective leaders as they confront the many challenges to higher education and strive to meet the needs of campus students, faculty, staff, leaders, and alumni. For those of us who cherish our college experience and want the same for our children and grandchildren, these are times that require new dimensions of leadership and governance. The questions for trustees are not whether higher education will be challenged, but how, and not whether higher education will continue to evolve, but how it will change and reform.

Chapter 1

Historical and Structural Framework of Governance

It is essential for trustees to know the history and purpose of their own institution, the history and dynamics of other institutions in their sector, the history of colleges and universities in the United States, the history of higher education as an enterprise, and the types of governing, advisory, and coordinating boards that exist.

Equipped with such knowledge, board members can serve effectively as stewards of a state-granted charter, advise the president, provide connections with the broader world, and help guide their institution through the challenges of demographic, economic, technological, and political dynamics that are sure to disrupt long-range plans. Knowing institutional and higher education history can give a board member confidence that challenges have been met before, that institutions are resilient and can change quickly and dramatically when needed, and that new initiatives and programs can be developed in response to societal needs. Board members will learn that some criticisms of higher education lack merit, whereas others are legitimate and should inspire action.

History and Mission of Higher Education

Each university has a unique story. Each was started by someone with a vision, each visionary had followers who believed in the vision, and each new institution had a context that often proved to be fertile ground for supporting the vision. The central mission of the university, which includes four-year and two-year colleges as well as doctoral and research institutions, is a dedication to the search for truth and the preparation of students as citizens and professionals. Institutions of higher education want graduates who are able to distinguish among empirical evidence, epiphanies or beliefs, and emotion, fear, or superstition. How this mission has been conceived and fulfilled depends upon the impulses and commitments of the founders and institutional leaders.

Was the institution created to serve the general public, prepare clergy or teachers, or enroll women, African Americans, and Jews denied access to other institutions? Was it intended to fulfill a federal mandate for population dispersal, to develop programs in scientific agriculture, or to meet the needs of emerging industries? Colleges and universities are distinguished by their founding characteristics, which were often influenced by population pressures, politics, and public investment in both charters and funding.

Harvard was founded in 1636 as the first college in the United States, with a mission to provide a "learned ministry" through the "transformative power of the arts and sciences."[1] Thomas Jefferson expanded beyond the limits of this "learned ministry" when planning the University of Virginia, founded in 1816. Jefferson was an early proponent of increased educational opportunity for the citizens of the state to support the nation's growing market economy and to meet the needs for advanced knowledge, skills, and abilities.

By 1861, there were more than 780 colleges in the United States, 182 of which survive to the present day. Of those remaining, most were founded as a direct response to the westward expansion of population and were religiously based, while only twenty-one were state or municipal colleges. In 1862, President Abraham Lincoln signed the Morrill Land-Grant Act to support the growth of scientific agricultural practices, which was reinforced by the Hatch Act of 1887.

The first grants of federal land were sold to the states in 1862 and used to start new schools or to fund existing state or private colleges. For most, the purpose was to create more schools of agriculture and mechanic arts in regions still being populated. The second Morrill Act of 1890 was enacted to create federal support for the admission of African Americans into institutions of higher education. The institutions created from this act are those now called historically black colleges and universities (HBCUs).

In the late nineteenth century, expansion of higher education began to include women as well. To name just a few examples, Adelphi University was founded in 1896 by a group of suffragists, abolitionists, and religious free thinkers who wanted to create a great university in Brooklyn with equal opportunity for men and women. (Unfortunately, the first African American was not admitted until 1947.) Wellesley College was founded in 1870 with a focus on the liberal arts to prepare "women who will make a difference in the world . . . not to be ministered to but to minister."[2] The University of Chicago was founded in 1890 to provide opportunities in all departments to students of both sexes. The City College of New York was started in 1847 as the Free Academy, where, the founders said, "The experiment is to be tried, whether the children of the people . . . can be educated and whether an institution of the highest grade . . . can be successfully controlled by the popular will, not by the privileged few."[3]

In 1901, the nature of higher education institutions evolved yet again as the first community college grew out of adult education programs at a high school in Joliet, Illinois. The network of public two-year colleges blossomed in the 1930s, flourished following the Truman Commission in 1948, and developed still further in the 1960s, with nearly 1,200 in operation by 2016.

Higher education also changed dramatically during and after the Second World War. At the beginning of the war, the federal government worked with universities to develop accelerated officer training programs on college campuses, and at the war's conclusion the government adopted the GI Bill of 1944, the Servicemen's Readjustment Act. This bill offered financial aid for veterans to attend college and encouraged colleges to expand in order to provide spaces for the incoming students. In the process, small, limited-mission liberal arts colleges expanded in scope and size, many becoming primarily pre-professional in their offerings, and former colleges founded with the intention to educate teachers became regional institutions with expanded missions for graduate study and research.

The characteristics of many colleges changed in response to these societal, political, and financial imperatives. This was especially evident in college admissions practices. The profile of students in officer candidate programs and the influx of veterans to colleges at the end of the war required changes in traditional policies and practices, and boards had to respond to these changes. In some cases, years of single-sex education were changed to coeducational almost overnight.

There is the frequent refrain that higher education in the United States had a "golden age" after the Second World War, when higher education was highly valued and supported by public policy. However, this claim dims if one considers the inadequate commitment to equality of opportunity and lack of racial, gender, and economic diversity, despite President Harry S. Truman's 1947 Commission on Higher Education for Democracy.

This report called for the elimination of racial and religious barriers to higher education. Even today, echoes of these barriers are evidenced in such statements as "Those kids don't need college," uttered by a legislator in Arizona in 2013 in response to a business group's advocacy for increased higher education funding.[4]

Higher education continued to change as we borrowed from examples in other countries and developed new models. It evolved from its historic role as the place and time when adolescents became adults. Many students no longer experienced a prolonged adolescence, but were already working adults. Colleges and universities responded to these and other societal needs by creating, revising, expanding, and eliminating subjects of study. They expanded in scale and scope, and became ever more central to society and the achievement of the American dream of individual progress. Small private colleges whose mission was to prepare clergy and teachers developed into major graduate universities dedicated to the preparation of other professionals as well as graduate education and scholarly research. Regional public and private colleges aspired to increase their commitments to research and scholarship by reducing teaching obligations, adding staff to support the pursuit of government and industrial grants, and changing the campus reward structure to honor publications and patents, sometimes to the detriment of commitments to undergraduate teaching. New forms of institutions, such as private, for-profit schools and community colleges, were created. Higher education became more of a "public good" than solely a matter of private gain.

Over the second half of the twentieth century, higher education continued to change in these and other ways:

- The proportion of enrollment at public institutions increased relative to that in private colleges and universities
- Academic programs with more emphasis on professional degrees at the undergraduate level were created

- Priority was given to graduate-level research and scholarship, relative to undergraduate teaching by the faculty
- Widening access to college for women, under-represented minorities, and those from low-income families was supported
- Federal, state, and institutional financial aid programs were developed
- Increased intensity of competition among campuses became the norm

Today, there are 1,985 public institutions of higher education in the United States, 1,876 private, nonprofit institutions, and almost 3,000 private, for-profit colleges. Forty percent of institutions enroll fewer than 1,000 students, while 80 percent enroll fewer than 5,000 students. There are more than 20 million students attending all types of colleges, including 17.5 million undergraduate students and nearly 3 million graduate students. Seventy-two percent of all students are attending public institutions. Women make up 56 percent of students enrolled in higher education. More than 9 million students receive federal, income-based Pell Grants intended for students from the lowest income families, with an average median family income under $30,000 per year and an average award of about $3,700.[5]

In recent decades, colleges and universities have been charged by governments, accrediting bodies, and philanthropic foundations with raising the priority of granting access to new populations of students from low-income families; improving affordability to support income diversity; and instituting stronger measures of accountability for the quality of academic offerings, the soundness of student learning, and the graduation rates of entering students. Especially at the undergraduate level, the goals of higher education have been to widen access to students of all ages and backgrounds, whether enrolled full-time or part-time, and promote excellence in teaching and research for the common good. A great variety of student counseling and academic support services, especially those related to mental health, have been developed to support student success, retention, and graduation. While these services have been moderately successful in raising overall graduation rates, they also have had the unfortunate effect of straining campus budgets.

At one time, it was thought that public higher education in the United States should be free through tax support, and for many years public higher education in California and New York City was tuition-free. Most other states charged only minimal fees. Since 2008, state funding for public universities has been cut by 28 percent, while tuition has increased an average of 27 percent. In Arizona and California, tuition has increased more than 70 percent. These cuts occurred during a period when there was general consensus that universal post-secondary education was more necessary than ever.[6]

State and federal student financial aid programs were not developed until the middle of the twentieth century. In earlier years, private institutions raised endowed and expendable funds to provide scholarship assistance for talented but needy students, especially for the children of clergy and teachers.

University and college presidents and boards should speak up for the historic values and purpose of higher education as a public good, and argue for the benefits of broadening access, maintaining affordability, and strengthening accountability measures. They must assert and demonstrate that mission-oriented higher education has been and continues to be of great benefit to society at large, as well as to students as individuals, especially during periods when attacks against colleges are pervasive. Among the most admirable features of American higher education are the historic focus on expanding opportunity for upward mobility, the institutional commitment to high-quality educational programs and student learning, governmental policies supporting higher education for a public purpose, private philanthropy promoting the advancement of the citizenry, and institutional missions serving a growing nation.

This understanding of history is intended to provide some perspective for meeting the challenges of today. While the Great Recession of 2008 was not as dire or as prolonged as the Great Depression of the 1930s, many consequences were similar. In the 1930s, state funding for higher education was cut by about 40 percent, and private college endowments dropped by more than 25 percent. Alumni and philanthropic giving fell by more than 70 percent. Faculty and staff salaries were reduced. Similar challenges to the purpose of college and calls for greater relevance in the curriculum were heard. Nevertheless, these resilient institutions survived, and academic freedom was largely preserved. Higher education has weathered periods of disruption and change in the past, and it has the capacity to do so again.[7]

Development of Board Governance

The role of governing boards has evolved from the time of small private colleges preparing clergy and teachers to the modern institutions of today. John Kirkpatrick's history of the formation of government at Harvard outlines the development of the governance structure that has become a model for many boards today.[8] At Harvard, the board developed from an original *in-residence* model consisting of five faculty members and the president to a *nonresident* form of government. After some decades, Harvard supplanted the faculty members of the board with clergy and then members of the community. In response to urging from the municipal government, Harvard also created a companion Board of Overseers in 1642. This board still serves a significant role in institutional governance, along with the President and Fellows, also known as the Corporation. Elected by degree holders from Harvard, the board of overseers consists of thirty members who advise but do not govern the university. Nearly four centuries later, the basic pattern established at Harvard has been adopted and modified throughout higher education.

Many public colleges have two boards, one for governing and one for external advice and fundraising. Most boards of trustees consist of members of the broader community, instead of members of the faculty. In only a few cases does the institutional president serve as chair of the board of trustees.

As institutions have responded to external pressures, their missions, enrollment challenges, and forms of governance have had to evolve. Colleges based in a religious tradition supplemented ministers and bishops as trustees with leaders from business and other professions. In the 1960s and 1970s, accrediting bodies and state education departments introduced requirements for board membership that further diluted connections with religious bodies.

In the 1970s, with federal support, states created higher education coordinating commissions intended to support statewide academic and facilities planning, reduce or limit the duplication of expensive or specialized degree programs, and preserve mission differentiation among both public and independent campuses. Coordinating commissions are not governing boards. They lack the legal authority to hire the president, set tuition, reallocate resources, or buy land. They are authorized to approve any new degree programs or degree levels for all institutions, except those created by a state's constitution and the federal government. These state coordinating boards, whose members are appointed by the governor, emphasize coordination and cooperation among public and private institutions in order to limit competition and duplication of effort so as to promote the effective and efficient use of public resources. However, state coordinating boards do not all execute their missions in the same manner.

Shifts in governmental involvement have changed the roles and responsibilities of many institutional boards of trustees.

Those responsible for trustee appointments should select members who are knowledgeable about the purposes of higher education and ideally are without an uncompromising ideology or partisan position. Public institution board members are usually appointed by the state's governor, often with approval by the legislature. This process can result in boards that are more ideological and intrusive because of public and political pressure on such issues as tuition levels, institutional spending, and student activism. (See Public Policy in chapter 2 for more information on the ways in which public policy and other governmental actions can influence governing decisions at institutions of higher education.)

The degree to which a board operates as a basic fiduciary agent or as a more strategic guide can vary. Variations include the self-perpetuating private institution board, the publicly elected or government-appointed public college board of trustees, advisory boards, and foundation boards. While most public and private colleges have local boards of trustees, some boards are responsible for governing multi-campus systems. Such systems may have multiple missions, with one or more campuses, including major research institutions, several regional campuses that are more oriented toward teaching but perhaps also include a research mission, some two-year or community colleges, and even an entirely online or distance education institution. In these instances, the leading research university is considered the flagship and may even have state constitutional status. In several dozen states, one campus is designated as the public liberal arts college, with a focus on undergraduate teaching and a strong grounding in the arts, humanities, sciences, and social sciences (even when professional programs like business and nursing are also offered). As some institutions evolve in emphasis from a focus on undergraduate teaching in a residential community to a priority for knowledge creation at the graduate level, or to serving a larger population of students through a system of nearly open admissions in which education becomes more of a commodity, the priorities of the board will change.

While the basic elements of governance are universal and continual, the degree of emphasis depends upon the mission of the institution and the forces at work at different times. The structure of board governance can change according to the push of institutional heritage and the pull of environmental forces. These forces include individual demands from students and their families, societal pressures, and the influence of both private and public patrons. The priorities of a governing board can change in response to a variety of academic, demographic, economic, or political imperatives. There could be a new or newly expanded commitment to a different population demographic, a new academic division created to serve a new region, or an existing academic unit newly dedicated to teaching at a distance. Perhaps there is a new initiative for "free" tuition at public institutions in the state, which can cause competitive challenges for private, tuition-dependent campuses, or there is need for a campus to contemplate a merger or even closure due to increasing debt and declining revenue. But before undertaking a merger or closure, a board might consider a strategic alliance with another campus, including joint degree programs, collaboration on "back-office" operations, joint purchasing, or other forms of alliance that maintain separate governing boards.

These are new demands on trustees. The need when contemplating closure is to admit the challenges, understand the market, be alert to the "canaries in the mine shaft," know the campus's legal options, and plan to preserve the memories of the campus as best one can.

Nevertheless, the principles of governance have continued to be honored even as they are adapted in response to the demands of the day. As institutions decide, with input from the faculty, how to address these challenges and others, decisions should be made by majority vote and with the board chair, in concert with the president, responsible for handling disagreements.

Shared Governance

While the board of trustees has ultimate authority, it explicitly delegates powers to the president as chief executive officer and to the faculty as guardians of academic programs and standards in a unique system known as *shared governance*. In 1966, the Association of Governing Boards of Universities and Colleges (AGB), the American Association of University Professors (AAUP), and the American Council on Education (ACE) issued a statement on the relative roles of trustees, campus presidents, and faculty in governing a university. Each has an important role to play in fulfilling the mission of an institution and must work with the others in order to develop the mutual respect and trust necessary to move the institution forward.

Shared governance is not without its challenges. One argument made against shared governance is that it slows down the process of decision-making, while another is that those sharing in governance do not share equally. There are patterns of institutional behavior as well as requirements of law that temper the possibility of sharing more fully. Because of this imbalance of power, there are some who have discarded the term *shared governance* in favor of the term *distributed governance*.

Conflicts during the process of shared or distributed governance may occur between faculty senates and boards regarding decisions about compensation and benefits or about the approval of new programs or courses. The prevalence of cases in which trustees remove presidents precipitously, appoint presidents without an adequate search, increase the number and proportion of contingent or part-time faculty, and reduce budgets because of shortfalls in state and tuition revenue without faculty consultation serve to undermine the ideal of shared governance on all campuses, not just those immediately affected.

As Jonathan Cole put it in his book *The Great American University*, university governance is "a mixture of authority, power, and persuasion by consent of the governed."[9] As the board guides an institution through the governance process, faculty must give their consent as the governed, while the president must lead with a mixture of authority, power, and persuasion within the context of the mandate given to the position. The shared governance process, through which trustees make decisions based on input from the president and faculty, takes place largely in committees.

Committees

Familiarity between the board members and all campus constituents is essential. It is also important for board members to become acquainted with the vice presidents, deans, and other important administrators, and to understand the responsibilities of these offices. The board should know these officials as individuals, so that presentations at board meeting can take place in a setting of mutual respect that acknowledges each person's role.

The Trustee Affairs Committee, sometimes known as the Governance or Nominating Committee, working with the board chair and the president, is responsible for helping make board service matter. This committee should arrange to rotate the membership and leadership of board committees so that individual trustees gain experience in the various dimensions of the university. Most work is done through committees, and rotating through them is necessary preparation for future leadership on the board. The committee system works best when there is sufficient trust among board members. If most of the work of the board is done in committee, then those not on the committee must trust that their responsibilities for oversight are not compromised.

Each committee should have a charter specifying the range of issues under its purview as well as specifications regarding the number of members and any special requirements desired. For example, the Finance Committee should include at least some members with financial literacy. Each committee should have a staff liaison as well as a senior officer assigned to it. As a good practice to sustain institutional knowledge, the board administrator, sometimes called the assistant secretary, should keep an inventory of "lessons learned" so that committees do not have to cover the same ground twice and can continue to make effective decisions that build on past work.

A committee's role is two-fold. First, it receives recommendations from the administration and reviews the processes followed to ensure that the campus is not legally liable for a violation of process. For example, the board can ask why the faculty vote on a candidate is mixed or why a candidate without the terminal doctoral degree is being recommended when this is usually not the case. Second, the committee reviews how recommendations fit in with the programmatic and financial plans for the university. For example, the granting of tenure represents a potential capital investment of close to $4 million over thirty or more years, counting salary and benefits if the starting amount is $100,000. Any multimillion-dollar capital investment would receive considerable discussion about the strategic issues involved and the alternatives considered. Therefore, the decision is not about the individual, but about the need for the position, the need for it in a particular department, and the processes followed in advancing the recommendation.

Some board members with a background in business may feel that they have no expertise in academia and so should not, for example, serve on the Academic Affairs Committee, which reviews the credentials of potential faculty members or candidates for tenure or promotion. However, the experience of these board members is valuable. As stated previously, their role is not to evaluate individual credentials but to review the strategic and legal (or procedural) issues related to an appointment to a tenure-track or tenured position. There often are legitimate questions about how the person recommended will help fulfill goals for enrollment, diversity, student advising, research revenue, and campus citizenship. This is the monitoring role of the committees and the board. Board members assist the chief academic officer and the president in ensuring that both plans and processes are monitored for strategic purpose, quality control, risk assessment, and financial stability.

Customary university board committees and their responsibilities include the following. Academic Affairs approves faculty appointments, promotion, and tenure based on a faculty staffing plan, as well as approving emeritus status for faculty and others qualified; the appointment of new deans as faculty members; and newly proposed academic programs, including "Pathway Programs" for international students. In addition, the committee reviews the periodic external reviews of academic programs and the one-year follow-up to the reviews; goals for diversity in academic staffing relative to goals for retention and graduation; draft and final accreditation self-studies; and other standards of quality assurance. In some cases, the Academic Affairs and Student Life Committees are combined into one committee, or the two committees have joint meetings once or twice a year because of overlap in the areas of concern.

The Advancement or Development committee's responsibilities include fundraising (annual giving, capital campaigns, and targeted fund drives), alumni relations, public and community relations, publications, and both internal and external communications.

The Audit committee monitors both internal and external financial audits and tax returns as well as internal operations audits; enterprise risk assessment measures, including trustee-to-trustee business connections; nepotism among employees or involvement of trustee relatives on campus; cyber-security and weather-related events, such as hurricanes, attempting to avoid the need for crisis management; whistle-blower hotline policies and procedures; and contracts over a certain size, as well as legal claims and union grievances. The Audit committee also reviews and approves any audit firm contracts.

The Buildings and Grounds committee oversees facilities maintenance, building renovation, and new construction; monitors depreciation; interviews prospective architects and construction managers; and monitors submissions to zoning, fire department, and other municipal boards.

The Finance and Administration committee oversees the treasury functions as well as the variety of personnel-related functions, including benefits, labor contracts, legal counsel, and federal compliance requirements, such as Title IX.

The Investment committee oversees the true endowment, which is donor-restricted in use, as well as unrestricted and undesignated funds functioning as endowment that are subject to board direction. This committee takes a long-term view on risk tolerance and institutional needs, and monitors policies that limit investment income eligible to be used in the annual operating budget, usually 5 percent of the rolling five-year average.

The Student Life committee's responsibilities include admissions and retention (although this is sometimes included under Academic Affairs), international student and visa administrative requirements, student government and other campus-life activities, residential life, dining services, events scheduling, athletics, the campus judicial system, and Greek life (fraternities and sororities). The National Collegiate Athletic Association (NCAA) recommends that the director of athletics should report directly to the president. However, institutions with smaller athletic programs may prefer to have the position report to the chief student affairs officer.

The Public Safety Office performs an essential campus service directly related to the quality of student life. The chief safety officer should be in direct communication with the chief student affairs officer, as public safety is highly related to student success. While public safety may fall under the purview of administration or maintenance and facilities, or even financial affairs, the chief safety officer should always maintain a strong and clear relationship with the offices responsible for student activities, athletics, residence life, dining, and related functions.

The Trustee Affairs committee, in addition to the duties already discussed, is responsible for the continuing professional development of the board, the designation of emeritus status for board members who successfully complete their prescribed term, and the annual board self-evaluation and evaluation of the board chair. The assistant secretary often serves as the specific liaison to the Trustee Affairs committee.

Most boards also have an Executive committee consisting of the officers, the heads of select committees, and a few at-large members. The Executive committee should not act for the full board unless a specific decision has been delegated to it. Some institution leaders think that an active Executive committee creates the impression of a two-tiered board. It is easy enough to hold a conference-call meeting of the full board about an urgent topic if this method of governance is preferred. The use of email ballots for periodic issues should be managed carefully.

Boards also appoint ad hoc committees for special purposes, such as to consider a multiyear plan for tuition and financial aid or to monitor collective bargaining by the human resources and finance staffs. In the latter case, it is better to have board involvement in the setting and monitoring of collective bargaining goals than for the president to present a fait accompli after the staff and union negotiators think they are finished, only to have the board balk at the terms.

The board chair may find it useful to call upon an Executive committee or an ad hoc committee consisting of the board officers and committee chairs as a sounding board for sensitive issues, such as the president's review, when not asking for a vote. In any case, it is essential to keep the full board informed about all discussions and decisions.

Some boards seek recent insights about campus life and increased diversity by creating a young alumni membership category. By including graduates from the past ten years, in staggered terms, but serving no more than three years each, the board can both benefit from a recent perspective on academic and student life at the campus and increase the chances for diversity in membership.

In order to recognize and retain the interests of helpful board members, boards use the title of *emeritus* or *emerita* to continue the relationship with a departing member who has earned the status. Such members may receive meeting materials and attend board meetings, but usually are limited in their degree of participation during discussions and votes.

Relationship with the President

The board of trustees is obligated to select a president. Campus presidents are variously described as chief narrators, budget masters, lobbyists, sales representatives, high-stakes "panhandlers," promoters, and entrepreneurs. These varied views of the college presidency may be especially true at public institutions of higher education, for in this sector the pressures are great for mass instruction in large classes and for specific career training. Rather than serving as a corporate-style CEO, the president should serve as the chief education officer, reminding students, faculty, staff, and alumni about the institution's heritage and purpose and leading the mandate from the board to fulfill agreed-upon strategies to achieve agreed-upon goals.

The board of trustees typically hires a president with responsibilities that are separate from the board chair but mutual in terms of overall goals. There are only a few examples of campus presidents who serve as both chief executive officer and board chair. Therefore, the board, and especially the board chair, should be the president's partner in establishing priorities and strategies in fulfillment of the institution's mission and the responsibilities for governing. With adequate information for the board to act in an informed way, many elements of the campus business or economic plan, as well as the broad responsibilities for quality control and effectiveness, will be understandable and open for review and refinement.

The president hires a senior staff to assist with campus leadership. These positions typically include a chief academic officer, sometimes called the provost, who is usually considered second in the line of authority. The chief financial officer (CFO) is either third in line or equal to the provost as an executive vice president. In addition, the president's senior staff will include a chief advancement or development officer, a chief enrollment management officer, a chief student affairs officer, and a senior officer responsible for internal and external communications. Such communications include electronic and print materials for advertising, marketing, news releases, and publications, as well as relations with various media outlets. In some cases, those responsible for communications will report to the chief development or institutional advancement officer, and enrollment management and student affairs will report to the provost. In a large institution, there also may be a vice president for facilities management and administration. The exact title for each position will vary by the size of the institution, but many carry the title of vice president.

After the board has hired a president and approved the appointments of senior officers and deans, members should agree on annual or multiyear goals for the administration and review progress annually, but they should not try to do the job of the campus executive. When this happens, a revolving door to the president's suite can be the result.

There is an old maxim about effective boards: *They keep fingers out but noses in*. That is, they do not get so close as to "touch" and manage the campus, but they get close enough, and informed enough, to "smell" anything not going well. Of course, individual members must be careful not to be viewed as snooping around or cultivating back-channel contacts that could undermine the effectiveness of the board and the president. They also need to be careful with how they use what they hear. If the information is sufficiently troubling, they should advise the president or the chair.

The campus presidency can be a lonely post, and board members play a critical role in sustaining the well-being of their chief executive. Not only is the presidency a "24-7" position, requiring a great deal of travel for alumni relations and fundraising, but it is also the recipient of all sorts of slings and arrows, including "out-of-the-blue" federal lawsuits, complaints about the hiring— or firing—of a coach, and campus tragedies, such as a fire or the death of a student. The board is obligated to support the president with adequate staff, professional development opportunities, mentoring, appropriate attention, and time for relaxation.

Ideally, boards should be partners with the campus president. Board members are expected to be experts in an area of concern to the institution without meddling in its affairs. Unfortunately, there are cases in which there is friction between the two parties. A strong partnership is essential in developing goals to fulfill the institutional mission and in monitoring the progress of strategic initiatives. However, not all boards adequately fulfill their responsibilities for overseeing standards, values, and finances. There are, unfortunately, examples of boards no longer acting as buffers against the media and other outside influences but that instead join those who buffet the administration. The chair must be the leader of the whole board, not of a faction, providing guidance for cohesion and consensus. The chair must encourage all to talk but be mindful of the board's responsibility to its duties and its purpose to help the university fulfill its mission in the most effective ways.

Chapter 2

Board Responsibilities

D avid Riesman, the renowned sociologist of higher education and society, is said to have described the role of the board as protecting the university of the future from the decisions of the present. This is sound advice.

University boards are different in many ways from other boards. They are different in their expectations of the organization's leader, the characteristics of their constituents, the context in which they lead, the expectations of their members, and the measurements of success. Trustees are accountable for higher education institutions' most fundamental principles: institutional autonomy and independence, the protection of academic freedom, and commitment to a public purpose.[1] They are responsible for institutions that are charged not only with preparing graduates for productive roles in society but also with questioning that same society.

This is as it should be, as the university's role is three-fold: creator, curator, and critic. In fulfillment of its mission of teaching, research, and service, the university serves as a creator of new knowledge and understanding. It is a curator of what is known, serving as a repository of the past. Finally, it is a critic of the status quo, emphasizing and supporting independent thought. A university education is, or should be, as much about character and citizenship as it is about careers and commerce.

While the board is responsible for guiding the fulfillment of the mission of its institution, the activities of a board are determined by the powers, duties, and responsibilities delegated to it or conferred on it by an authority outside of itself. In the case of higher education institutions, that authority is either the state government or the state constitution. Therefore, boards are responsible for fulfilling state law and must be prepared to do so. College and university trustees hold an institution's state-granted charter in trust. This means that they are legally entrusted with the institution's care and are subject to certain formal obligations and duties in order to protect it for the benefit of others. They are stewards for all aspects of the enterprise, even for those parts that they delegate to others. In fulfilling this role, they have the traditional board duties of care and loyalty, but also an extra duty of obedience to mission that is essential to all nonprofit boards.[2]

The duty of care relates to the level of competence expected of the board in carrying out governance responsibilities by using the degree of diligence and skill one would expect of a prudent person fulfilling such an assignment. It is the duty to participate actively in governance, to protect the institution through appropriate oversight, and to identify and manage risks.

The duty of loyalty requires that board members act in good faith and in the best interests of the institution, not out of self-interest. This duty specifies that a trustee should not have mixed loyalties, but pledge allegiance to just one institution at a time. This duty is the basis for avoiding conflicts of interest.

The duty of obedience requires that board member actions must be true to the campus charter and act to fulfill it in a manner that complies with the law and furthers the stated mission of the institution. This duty is based on the premise that constituents and the public at large can trust that what they are told by the board is true.

The university board should adopt and follow a statement of expectations that serves as a compact between each member and the board itself as well as with the institution. The best board practices can be found in many institutions, whether small liberal arts colleges, community colleges, major research universities, or state-wide systems of public institutions. Each board and member must fulfill the duties of care, loyalty, and obedience, no matter what the size or the mandate of the institution. The board sets the standards for institutional deliberations. It can support a culture of respect and transparency, or one of secretiveness. Transparency is necessary for trust, and both are essential for good governance.

Some boards may engage a consultant for guidance in establishing best practices for board governance. The Association of Governing Boards of Universities and Colleges (AGB) is a helpful resource for finding experienced and knowledgeable experts in the field. AGB also has consultancies in coaching senior campus leaders and in providing interim presidents. These practices grew out of their successful work in helping campuses search for presidents, provosts, and deans, a practice that in turn grew from their guidance on trustee governance.

In addition to protecting the cultural essence of the institution, the role of board members also is financial. According to the AGB, nearly 81 percent of private nonprofit institutions report that 90 to 100 percent of board members make a financial commitment to the college, while less than one half (44.3%) of public respondents report the same.[3] However, while trustees are expected to serve as boosters and donors, they also have a much broader role. Too often, boards are composed with fundraising instead of governance in mind. The university board's responsibilities include giving priority to mission and purpose, as well as to balancing instruction, scholarship, and service to the broader community.

AGB identifies the basic duties of a board as the following:

- Ensuring the integrity of the mission
- Guarding academic quality, institutional autonomy, and academic freedom
- Guarding fiscal integrity
- Engaging effectively and appropriately with students, faculty, staff, alumni, and the community
- Selecting, supporting, assessing, and compensating the president
- Overseeing strategic planning
- Regularly assessing board performance, policies, and practices[4]

Ensuring the Integrity of the Mission

The campus mission statement is the institutional expression of educational values, goals, and outcomes; it expresses the campus vision and purpose. Annual academic program and administrative unit reviews should always refer to the mission statement and strategic plan, thus providing an opportunity to assess the degree to which the programs and units support institutional goals and objectives related to student success and other institutional aspirations.

Universities are moral institutions in that they can be exemplars of what is good and ethical as well as what is bad and fraudulent. Universities demonstrate their values by their actions as well as by what is taught in the classroom. Institutional behavior includes accommodations for those who need special considerations, construction practices, investment policies, academic freedom in the pursuit of knowledge, and support of student success. Institutions of higher education have an obligation to be honest, given their unique role in society, yet we know that some campuses fudge the numbers when it comes to reporting average SAT scores or the percentage of alumni who participate in annual giving, for example. Others have used misleading photographs and text in brochures and online to promote themselves. These issues should be of concern to board members.

Board members should help guide their institution away from reputational risk. Unfortunately, we have seen many cases of boards and presidents suffering negative press in the headlines of both local and national news stories, often in relation to a campus controversy. Therefore, reputational risk should be included in the campus enterprise risk analysis and cover not only topics such as fraud, including academic fraud involving athletics, financial misdeeds, and the risks inherent in study abroad programs, but also topics such as the ethical use of student data and human subject research. The enterprise risk policy also should provide guidelines for handling responses to inquiries and informing key constituents about any incidents, if such information can be verified, as faulty or delayed responses and mixed messages can make matters worse.

Other ethical issues are related to conflicts of interest among board members or connected to board members receiving contracts as vendors. Does the board member who recommends an investment have an ownership stake in the company? Does the board member who advocates a specific "no-fail" opportunity have a personal relationship with the investment manager? Are his or her investments on the same or similar terms to those being recommended for the university? Will the trustee advocating the investment agree to an independent analysis of the manager? If not, beware. Remember, the Bernard Madoff investment scandal involved university boards as well as individual investors.

While some of these concerns have been evident in board service for many years, others are new, and still others will evolve. This is why it is important for the board's audit committee to guide the full board in enterprise risk analysis, including such topics as board member-to-member relationships on and apart from the board. The analysis should include routine reviews of the institution's officers and directors insurance coverage. The goal is to plan for and minimize risk; it cannot be avoided entirely.

Examples of risk and ethical challenges include student attrition and debt default rates, fraud in research due to the relationship between the scholar and the sponsor, violations of intellectual property rights and plagiarism by officials, failure to respond to a crisis or troubling event in a timely manner, endangering the stability and sustainability of the institution or individuals, pension and healthcare liabilities, and student misconduct, among other examples.

Because of the many personnel and contractual matters on the board's agenda, colleges and universities engage lawyers. Some hire in-house counsel to advise the president and the board, and to coordinate any outside counsel. Some boards even have their own counsel for especially complicated matters.

Other institutions rely on an outside firm with a range of legal talent to serve the role of general counsel and then hire one or more separate firms for specific, highly specialized matters, such as labor negotiations. These days, most institutions have a Title IX coordinator who reports to the president, the CFO, or human resources, and they increasingly hire lawyers specifically to manage responses related to this federal mandate regarding gender discrimination and sexual assault.

There can be ambiguity and uncertainty in board service, even as there are cycles of seemingly routine decisions about personnel appointments and performance reviews. Some of the ambiguous and uncertain matters confronting boards relate to ethical and legal issues, which are numerous and increasing. These include affirmative action as a federal policy, policies regarding transgender persons, and considerations for those who are hearing or sight-impaired or on the autism spectrum. The laws and regulations regarding accommodations are increasingly challenging, even as universities try to keep up and do the right thing.

Accreditation

An important responsibility of boards relates to accreditation, an essential form of quality control. Standard 4 of the *Standards for Accreditation and Requirements of Affiliation* of the Middle States Commission on Colleges and Universities is the touchstone for the topics of leadership and governance with regard to regional accreditation. It states, "The institution is governed and administered in a manner that allows it to realize its stated mission and goals in a way that effectively benefits the institution, its students, and the other constituencies it serves."[5]

All institutions must be accredited in order for students to qualify for federal financial aid, and most institutions offer academic degree programs that require programmatic accreditation. Seven regional accrediting bodies review campus self-studies on a periodic basis, usually five and ten years. The accrediting group engages educators from noncompeting institutions to analyze the institutional self-study; interview trustees, faculty, staff, students, and alumni about campus goals, processes, and progress; and write a report to the campus and the accrediting group. Accreditations for professional programs like business, chemistry, education, law, medicine, nursing, psychology, social work, and some other fields occur on different schedules, but follow basically the same model.

Accreditation is important for competitive reasons as well as for quality assurance and licensure. The accreditation of health programs is the most important and is necessary for graduates to qualify for licensing exams and gain employment. However, some accreditations are less essential; for example, many employers do not insist on recruiting only from accredited business programs. It is important for boards to balance the costs and benefits of professional accreditations, which can help student and faculty recruitment, but may add substantially to the costs of education.

In addition to regional and programmatic accreditations as forms of quality control, campuses engage outside experts from academia and industry to perform academic program reviews on a regular cycle. Institutions also engage in quality control efforts by scheduling operations audits of administrative units by the internal auditor or by outside consultants; talking with employers and graduate school admission deans about the preparation of students; and seeking arboretum status for the campus grounds or museum status for the art collection.

While not accreditation bodies, publications such as the *Fiske Guide to Colleges* and The Princeton Review's *Best Colleges* guide attempt to report on the quality of the student learning experience on the campuses covered. The popular *U.S. News & World Report* college rankings are based more on input data, such as acceptance rates and subjective popularity reviews, than on data that reflect the environment for learning and the results of faculty teaching. In the *U.S. News & World Report* rankings, the highest weight factor is the number of college presidents, provosts, and admission officers who rank an institution highly, which assumes that those who serve as judges actually know about the campuses they are asked to assess.

Outside groups may also publicize findings they assert are evaluations of colleges and their educational offerings. One such organization is the American Council of Trustees and Alumni (ACTA). This group gives priority to a more traditional or conservative approach to studies in American history and civilization, and publishes a report grading colleges based on whether their degree programs and general education requirements match the priorities of the organization.

Enrollment

A board's responsibilities for *guarding academic quality, institutional autonomy,* and *academic freedom* reach beyond accreditation. For example, boards should maintain a focus on the institution's mission even when promoting strategies to increase enrollment. The primary mission of the institution is academic (i.e., student learning and graduation), even as the institution needs to meet enrollment goals and support the fiscal bottom line. Boards should be aware of national and local changes in student interests and enrollment trends, and the effects they may have on institutions.

In fall 2015, more than 50 percent of private colleges suffered a decline in enrollment, and many also suffered a decline in net revenue.[6] It is important for the board to pay as much attention to graduate enrollment as it does to undergraduate enrollment, even though the latter gets more attention in the media and national reports. In order to fulfill their duties, board members should expect to receive timely and accurate information, such as the following:

- Number of applications for admission as well as information on changes in feeder (secondary) schools
- Demographic characteristics of students who apply, are offered admission, and enroll
- Discount rates for freshmen, transfers, and graduate students
- Retention rates from year to year
- Other metrics related to enrollment strength

To assist in recruiting desired students, universities create scholarships by discounting tuition. Unfortunately, the tuition discounting approach rarely allows room for institutions to increase the scholarship year after year in line with tuition increases. This can have negative effects on both retention rates and student indebtedness.

The term *discount rate* is often misunderstood. Some decades ago, in an effort to create scholarships when endowment income was not sufficient to do so, colleges adopted what was labeled a "high tuition-high aid" admissions and financial aid strategy to support need-based scholarships, supplement government grants, and provide merit-based financial aid awards to students with particularly desirable attributes, whether a strong passing arm or high SAT scores. Under this approach, all students are charged a higher tuition "sticker" price so that some students may receive a discount on their tuition bill. The discount is then called a scholarship. This form of institutional grant aid has become the primary source of student funds since 2011-12, and the use of student loans has declined, according to the National Association of Independent Colleges and Universities.[7] Nevertheless, we know that both parents and prospective students are concerned about projected costs.

As more and more colleges have adopted tuition-discounted scholarship aid to recruit students, the effect has been to drive up the level of discount, which for some colleges is bordering on unsustainable. This was one of the stated reasons for trustees at Sweet Briar College in Virginia to vote to stop enrolling students and close.[8] Colleges need to increase funding for endowed and expendable scholarships, and do more to reduce and control costs through the efficient and effective use of resources in order to ensure adequate net tuition income.

The board must make decisions about strategy and mission fulfillment related to student enrollment, ranking, and measures of success. There are many criticisms of ranking schemes that emphasize input measures, such as student SAT scores and subjective evaluations of quality. It is interesting to note that there is a movement underway to reduce or make optional standardized admissions tests like the SAT. There are several reasons for a campus to take such a decision. In some cases, the college may believe that talented student prospects are not applying because they think their scores are too low. In other cases, the institution may believe that college-guide reporting of SAT scores is hurting the institution's competitive profile. Finally, the institution may know that SAT scores are not highly correlated with student success and therefore decide not to require them. Some new rating measures have been developed to assess student outcomes, including such indicators as graduation rates, job placement, loan repayment rates, and salary information. While these are enhancements to the kind of information available to students and families to make an important decision, they still do not evaluate student learning.

Some enrollment management programs designed to enroll a diverse student body require support for students with academic and leadership potential who may be lacking the scholastic preparation necessary to gain normal admission. Such opportunity programs for domestic students are often labeled "remedial" because they are designed to remediate the shortcomings left from inadequate high school preparation. These programs also help adult students who left high school a decade or more ago to polish and enhance basic skills in math, writing, and reading that they have not used routinely. The level and kind of remediation varies by the institution and its requirements. If the basic freshman mathematics course is calculus, even talented students from resource-rich high schools may need a preparatory course. In most cases, though, remediation is for language and computational skills and is supplemented with required tutorials and advising.

There also are programs for students ready to accelerate. These include articulation agreements between four-year and two-year colleges that have coordinated their degree requirements so that a student who starts at a partner community college can transfer seamlessly to the four-year college. Colleges also have created early degree programs in high schools so that select students can take college-level courses taught by specially selected teachers, allowing students to earn both high school and college credit simultaneously. In addition, there are dual degree and accelerated 4 + 1 degree programs that allow college students to earn two degrees either simultaneously or in quick consecutive order.

Community college boards in particular should be knowledgeable about new competency-based credentials that are proposed as alternatives to credit-hour courses and degrees. These are being advocated as ways for preparing students more quickly for new jobs, and some are effective. It is worthwhile for four-year colleges and universities also to explore new credentialing options, including two-year degrees, certificate programs, and other "mini" degree approaches. Many university adult baccalaureate programs offer an associate degree option, for example, which can serve as career ladder for those with the Licensed Practical Nurse (LPN) designation. This allows these professionals to earn an associate degree in nursing and then advance to a bachelor's degree. Other possibilities include using the results of American Council on Education test results and College Learning Education Program (CLEP) exams to grant credit for life experiences. These are legitimate ways for colleges to help students document their learning, no matter where and how learned; be more efficient in their use of time and tuition dollars; and accelerate the time to graduation.

For some colleges, international students represent an important source of revenue due to declines in the domestic population in certain regions of the country. There are over one million students from other countries studying in the United States, accounting for about 5 percent of total enrollment. Nearly 60 percent of these students come from China, India, Saudi Arabia, and South Korea, and one-third enroll to study engineering, math, or computer science. It is estimated that international students contribute more than $35 billion annually to the U.S. economy.[9] Nevertheless, there are some admissions officers who warn of an international student "bubble" that could burst due to political concerns about the United States, changes in immigration policies, and ethical issues with foreign student recruitment.[10]

For international students, the basic preparatory course is English. The largest such provider is ELS-Berlitz, which partners with institutions across the United States to recruit students from other countries for English study and preparation for higher education studies. The level of English required for admission to undergraduate and graduate study varies by institution; those concerned about graduation rates set a higher bar. For those who are focused more on recruitment than on retention goals, the threshold for admission may be lower. However, it is often the case that faculty complain about too many students in a class for whom English is difficult, thus reducing the level of instruction for all students.

In recent years, private-sector providers have created so-called pathway or conditional programs designed to respond to both these faculty concerns and the administration's desire for more enrollment. In these cases, the campus and the private-sector firm create a joint venture organization that recruits the students, pays for the English language instruction, and arranges for the students to take some degree-credit classes while simultaneously improving their language skills. These programs are still new, and the graduation rates for students in such programs is not known. The model does seem to increase enrollment, although at a higher cost per student than the traditional ELS-Berlitz arrangement. It is not yet known how sustainable this approach is for the long term, given the amounts of money that the private-sector firms charge, which can be as much as $8,000 per student. In some cases, the firm takes 80 percent of the student fees, but it also is true that the pricing arrangement is highly variable.[11]

Student success should remain the goal even while increased enrollment to support the fiscal bottom line is the aim. The role of the board is to help guide campus leaders as they make decisions that require balancing the multiple priorities unique to institutions of higher learning. Ultimately, the university board holds an institution in trust, with a publicly granted charter. Its role, as David Riesman so aptly put it, is to protect the university of the future from the actions of the present. But to do so, the board must understand its duties of care, loyalty, and obedience, and know about the institution's purpose, strengths, and competitive forces in order to assist the campus in fulfilling its core missions of teaching, scholarship, and service.

Guarding Fiscal Integrity

The fiduciary duties of a board require it to focus on strategic and long-term issues and on the intersection of internal and public interests, something that presidents and faculty are not always able to do on their own. University and nonprofit boards are guided by state-approved charters and mission statements, and generally focus on ensuring the integrity of the mission, raising the resources necessary to support activities that are designed to fulfill the mission. The nonprofit board is not allowed to take a corporate-style or institutional position on political issues or attempt to impose its beliefs on others, even when pressed to do so by constituents. For-profit boards, on the other hand, may take political positions and contribute to political campaigns and candidates.

Comparisons between university and corporate boards, and criticisms of both, are not new. Charles W. Eliot, legendary president of Harvard, wrote in 1908 that "trustees are not themselves expert in any branch of the university teaching, and they are not experts in the policy or disciplines of the university."[12] Distinguished economist Thorstein Veblen's *The Higher Learning in America: A Memorandum on the Conduct of Universities by Business Men* was published in 1918. In it, he analyzed the differences between the governance of universities and the leadership of competitive businesses. Veblen was one of a number of university faculty members who criticized the governance of universities by people from business. While business structures generally adhere to a single bottom line as the priority, universities and nonprofits have multiple bottom lines. These include the interests of the students, faculty, employers, and other constituents they serve.

The university horizon is long term, while a private business, unless it is family owned, generally operates with a short-term horizon. This perspective affects the approach to developing new programs in the university, which expects a long life, as compared with new products at a firm, which requires a fast payback. A university is often concerned if its financial surplus is too large, while a for-profit business attempts to maximize profit. Nevertheless, a university should have incentives to save and not just spend an unbudgeted surplus that could be used for a one-time capital improvement or added to the funds functioning as endowment.

Corporate boards are equally accountable to the duties of care and loyalty, but they are not especially better in their execution. One need only ask what the boards of AIG and Lehman Brothers knew about their business models before the firms faced ruin, or what the boards of General Motors and Volkswagen knew about business practices intended to save money that resulted in deadly car crashes or a damaging bypass of federal environmental regulations by electronic cheating. These boards may have fostered corporate cultures that promoted short-term results rather than long-term gains.

Similarly, we may consider the example of Theranos, a blood testing company that imploded. When a Silicon Valley venture funder was asked by a *New York Times* reporter why he had not invested in the company, he said that the composition of the board had given him pause. The high-profile members of the board he mentioned were iconic national figures, but knew nothing about the technological basis for the company, had no experience in its market, and did not understand the product's competitive advantage.[13] In a similar example from the public sector, a Washington reporter writing in 2016 about forty years of woes within the Washington, DC, metro system indicated that the system's board had no coherent governance system and members lacked expertise in mass transit.[14]

These board members may have possessed individual expertise, but seem to have lacked the capacity or willingness to consider short-term risks and long-term consequences, or to be curious and ask necessary questions when in the group. Some boards get caught in a cycle of "Denial, Delay, and Defensiveness," as outlined by Deloitte's Center for Board Effectiveness.[15]

These boards, like too many others, seem to have lacked the "virtuous cycle of respect, trust, and candor"[16] necessary in a high-functioning board to ask probing questions in a manner of mutual respect, thus offering dissent without being disloyal.

University trustees need to know about the complexities and "messiness" of higher education financing, quality controls, government regulations, competition, tuition pricing, financial aid policies, international student recruitment, and so on if they are to be effective in their role. Universities operate under what are called *fund accounting* rules. Fund accounting emphasizes accountability rather than profitability and records resources according to their source, such as tuition, government grants, gifts, and so on, as well as their use. Colleges, generally, were created to promote particular priorities and interests that are reflected in both their funding sources and their expenses.

An issue that can rise to the level of concern for trustees involves investment fund policy. In the mid-1980s, college boards were lobbied to forego investments in South Africa as a protest against the system of apartheid. Today, students and other advocates argue against investments in coal, oil, natural gas extraction, liquor and beer, and tobacco. What is the board to do? Investing is behavior, and it is often argued that institutional behavior should model ethical behavior. Advocates may call for investing in alternative energy sources, such as solar and wind, instead of in coal and tar sands, and for avoiding investments in tobacco, but these investment choices may not produce the financial returns needed to support the campus. Most campuses include in their operating budgets about 5 percent or so of the five-year rolling average of investment income, with the wealthiest institutions including even more; some fund 30 percent or more of their operating budgets from investment returns. Clearly, the board has ethical choices to make when it comes to investment strategies and balancing goals for financial returns with goals such as environmental sustainability. Consider the conflict in having a campus goal for reducing the carbon footprint in operations and construction, but a policy that allows investing part of the endowment in coal and gas extraction.

Every discussion of finances and budgets should include an analysis of the institution's revenues and expenditures over time and in comparison to other institutions. The chief financial officer is responsible for managing the budget, although an audit firm can help. By comparing the ratio of revenues and expenditures over time and in comparison to both peer and aspirational institutions, board members and campus leaders can have a better understanding of the university's financial situation, including the following:

- Revenue diversity, including not only tuition but also investment, intellectual property, and real estate income
- Expense and financial aid ratios, separating out instruction, research and public service, academic support, student services, institutional support, auxiliary operations, and institutional financial aid
- Debt ratios, including debt service burden and average age of plant in years
- Liquidity ratios, especially in relation to operations and debt
- Full-time equivalent (FTE) student ratios to revenue and expenses by category

One list to avoid being on is the federal *Heightened Cash Monitoring* list of institutions in financial difficulty. The U.S. Department of Education requires these institutions to undergo additional oversight of cash management related to a number of financial or federal compliance issues. Not only do institutions that are being monitored often not have access to the advance payment method for drawing down federal financial aid for eligible students, but also their status is seen as a warning sign to credit agencies. Some institutions in this situation may consider merging with another or changing their mission in order to gain greater financial stability and maintain recruitment results.

Selecting, Supporting, Assessing, and Compensating the President

An annual review of the president is important; such evaluations should be clear and open, and occur before a crisis appears. They should be purposeful, rather than sudden decisions made because some trustee thinks that the president is not moving as fast as he or she thinks is appropriate in adopting a new technology or strategic direction. In addition to selecting the president, the board is responsible for nurturing the president's professional development, including leadership skills and abilities. (For a helpful guide, please see the Performance Review of the President template in Appendix A.)

Together with the president, the board should do the following:

- Set goals for the year for enrollment, the financial aid tuition discount rate, net tuition revenue, graduation rates, and the quality of results, among others
- Establish key metrics and milestones for the review of progress against goals
- Provide an annual written performance review after discussion with the president about his or her annual report for the year
- Recommend any changes in goals, expectations, compensation, and perquisites

The president's annual report should cover not only the goals and accomplishments for the year, but also responsibilities taken beyond the campus. Boards should support presidents who become active in community organizations related to the goals of the campus and who write articles or give interviews on issues related to higher education. While there are some metrics for measuring a president's performance, such as enrollment and net income, there are other areas of responsibility for which there are no clear measures of success. In some cases, such as relations with the faculty and students, success can be assessed only as a lack of failure.

"Boardroom battles" occur in two situations. The first happens when presidents take actions or behave in ways that faculty or members of the board find unacceptable. These actions often are related to fiscal matters, disagreements with the faculty, athletic scandals, or student unrest. The second occurs when there is board behavior that damages relations with the president, within the board, and with campus constituents. Troubling board behaviors include conducting secret sessions, leaving the president out of key discussions and decisions, engaging in conflicts of interest like ensuring that a relative is hired or interfering with an admissions decision, prejudging a situation based on outside and possibly biased and incorrect information, pleading for special interests, speaking for the board when not authorized to do so, and revealing confidential information.

From time to time, a board will have to deal with two areas of controversy: votes of no confidence taken by the faculty against the president, and a letter to the whole board from an angry alumnus or neighbor, or an anonymous source, alleging behavior unbecoming a president. When the faculty threatens or takes a vote of no confidence in a president, boards often react by declaring their support for the president. This lockstep approach of support may be a mistake. Instead, when controversy strikes, whether by faculty action or a letter of complaint, it is better to try to understand the origins of the complaint, identify the cause, and deal with the cause rather than immediately defend the president. To do so might make the president and not the issue the focus of attention. After all, the issue might be the result of a misinformed or malicious complaint or poor communication.

It is normal for a board to want to defend the president from criticism, and it makes sense for the board to do so, at least in private. But when the board's public response to known or anonymous criticism of the president is to defend him or her, it can exacerbate the controversy. The board's response should focus on the issue, not the personalities. In fact, it is sometimes the case that faculty ire with the president is actually caused by actions of the board.

The president should consult with the board chair and other officers, as well as perhaps an attorney, about a strategy for response. In responding to a letter, such a strategy might include a warning about defamation and slander. Campus leaders should avoid escalating the tension before understanding it. For a vote of no confidence to occur, there probably has been a monumental failure in communication, which can happen at an institution of any size. It is not unique to those that are large and complicated.

How do presidents get in trouble? Let us count the ways. Some fail because they think success is the result of their own actions and not those of a team. Egotism is readily detected and disliked. Then there are structural renovations and decorative refinements to the presidential residence. These are often reasons for complaint, as are bonus payments or special loans to the president or senior officers. Such actions become especially problematic when academic budgets are being cut, with concerns about finances used as the reason. Sometimes presidents get in trouble because they are carrying out the orders of the board when revenue has declined, expenses have risen, and the board does not want to see across-the-board cuts.

A president spending lavishly at his or her residence, on the office, or at restaurants will also raise the ire of campus constituents, as will the use of institutional money to pay for personal trainers or family travel. At least one president has gotten into trouble by appointing his spouse to an unofficial position that challenged the authority of existing senior staff. Another moved the general counsel from the office adjacent to the president to a distant location so the president's spouse could have the office near the presidential suite. Some presidents have gotten into trouble because they added administrative staff when faculty lines were frozen, or when a long-term, loyal, and well-known staff member was replaced by someone from the new president's previous institution. Others have gotten into trouble by hiring the relative of a trustee who later had to be fired, by interfering with the admission of an applicant endorsed by a trustee or the state governor, or by firing a coach favored by fans.

Erratic behavior; offensive comments about students, faculty, or staff; mishandling sexual assault and harassment allegations; being aloof from discussions of free speech and speech codes; or seeming to ignore racial incidents are additional reasons for presidents to be criticized. It is wise to be upfront with reporters, or even to call an editor and discuss an incident "off the record" before agreeing to do so on the record.

In some cases, campus presidents are invited to serve on corporate boards and receive additional compensation. While board service can contribute to the president's professional development, and academic presidents can contribute to the success of both for-profit and not-for-profit board governance, presidents should be judicious in their time commitments. This is especially true for those early in their tenure at a new institution. If the corporate board is located in a distant city, the number of days required for board service can mount up when one includes time for preparation, meetings, and travel. We have seen unflattering news stories and critical newspaper editorials about the amount of money earned and the number of days taken from campus duties by campus presidents serving on corporate boards. The troubles can be doubled if the time away does not result in funding for institutional projects.

Many times presidents get in trouble because the board has not been clear in expressing its expectations, or because powerful board members decide that there are new and emergent priorities that should take precedence over current plans. Poor and inadequate communications between the board and the president, and poor judgment by one party or the other, are often the reasons for trouble. The challenges can be great, but the characteristics of effective board-president relations are known. The boards that demonstrate this and nurture presidential leadership can help guide their institutions and campus leaders through challenging times.

Engaging with Faculty

The faculty as a collective are responsible for the four "essential freedoms" of a university, as enunciated by Justice Felix Frankfurter in the *Sweezy v. New Hampshire* Supreme Court case.[17] This 1957 case involved the state government attempting to curtail Professor Sweezy's speech by claiming it to be subversive, while Sweezy claimed that he had academic freedom speak what he considered to be the truth. This case affirmed academic freedom and empowered faculty to determine who may teach, what may be taught, how it shall be taught, and who may be admitted to study.

Faculty members play a particularly important role in planning, including overall strategic planning, academic planning, and facilities planning. They also should play an active role in responding to funding shortfalls, but too often do not want to make recommendations on what to cut. Including faculty in the decision-making process may help to address specific priorities, such as the inclusion of student advising as an explicit part of teaching, graduation rates, or supervised, credit-bearing internships for all students. When an institution is concerned about enrollment and finances, it should not at the same time spend money in ways that seem antithetical to academic interests without some discussion with the faculty. These responsibilities of the faculty require their specific attention, with both administrative and trustee support.

Fulfilling the responsibilities of the faculty for governance is among the reasons why it is important to have a sufficient cadre of full-time faculty and why tenure is an important personnel policy. Nevertheless, we can see shifts in certain aspects of faculty careers, with many institutions changing their reward systems to give more weight to teaching and advising and less weight to outside supported research and peer-reviewed publications. Some institutions even make this shift over the course of a faculty member's tenure, recognizing that research and other scholarly and creative breakthroughs often come early in a career. When making decisions regarding faculty, board members should consider whether campus policies reward or discourage teaching undergraduates.

One of the great ironies of collegiate life is that faculty are often rewarded for doing less of that which is central to the institution's mission (i.e., teaching and advising students). However, the irony can be understood when we realize that a faculty member's personal priority is control over his or her time to pursue activities that will most likely lead to the rewards of tenure and promotion. For this reason, boards and presidents must work to align institutional priorities and the reward system.

A concern for boards and presidents is the criticism about tenure and its presumed costs. This, too, is a topic that has grown in complexity over the years, even though the system of tenure was started as a protection against trustees and others wanting to control what faculty members taught. Tenure was developed as a means of providing employment protection for faculty members against those who disagreed with certain academic views and as a protection for faculty members to pursue "truth" in ways that might be counter to current wisdom. In the intervening years, public policies have been upgraded, and freedom of speech has been codified into law. Nevertheless, both academic freedom and tenure are both still needed, even if both are questioned.

In some cases, the campus response to funding shortfalls is to decrease the percentage of full-time faculty by replacing them with part-time or adjunct faculty. Adjunct, or contingent, faculty who fulfill niche roles or offer specific expertise not found on the full-time faculty, or expertise not needed full-time, can be valuable assets to a college. However, attempting to save money by increasing the number of adjunct or so-called contingent faculty also decreases the number of faculty who are accountable for academic quality and student advising. After all, a faculty focus on teaching is related not only to student success, but also to how high schools view the institution and how alumni remember it.

Some argue that including campus faculty membership on the board may be a challenge because their service as trustees would be limited; they may not be able fully to abide by the duties of care, loyalty, and obedience because they would represent particular constituencies. This is especially true at institutions with collective bargaining units for faculty. Even trustees elected by alumni bodies can be of concern if they are beholden to the body that elected them.

In the United States, some 21 percent of all colleges and universities have faculty unions, while about 35 percent of public institutions have them. According to the *Directory of U.S. Faculty Contracts and Bargaining Agents in Institutions of Higher Education*, nearly 370,000 faculty members belong to almost 640 bargaining units on about 1,200 campuses. The majority of unionized faculty is in California, New York, and New Jersey.[18] In addition to faculty unions, there are campus unions for graduate students; clerical workers; maintenance, engineering, and housecleaning staffs; public safety officers; and dining service workers, although not on all campuses. Each collective bargaining agreement must be approved by the board.

Collective bargaining units for faculty have been in existence since at least the 1970s, with some organized as local branches of the national American Association of University Professors (AAUP). Others are affiliated with the American Federation of Teachers (AFT). In recent years, we have witnessed a growing interest in collective bargaining units for graduate students. It is wise for boards to consult with legal experts on the prospects and implications of such actions.

It is always essential for the board and president to maintain open and respectful communication with the union president and vice president, as well as with any other student or faculty interest groups on campus. However, the separation between collective bargaining interests and faculty governance responsibilities should be maintained. Board members should treat all members of the faculty with respect and careful consideration. Uncivil behavior is noticeable and does harm to the very notion of governance, much less shared governance.

The faculty senate president or chairperson could meet with the academic affairs committee and the full board in all but executive sessions in order to foster communications. The board also can invite faculty to attend lunch or dinner in order to foster open discussions and good relationships. Board meetings (except for any executive sessions) could be held in public places so they are open for all to observe. Boards should be aware that one institutional barrier affecting shared governance with faculty is the academic calendar. Colleges and universities are year-round enterprises, yet the calendar for faculty governance is usually limited to nine or ten months (August or September to May). This limited calendar can present challenges for board and faculty relationships.

For effective shared governance, the relationship between president and faculty must be carefully cultivated. Faculty members have prerogatives, and a tenured full professor has a great deal of freedom to express opinions. However, most faculty members are reasonable. A university or college requires a form of covenant between the faculty and the president, just as there needs to be one between the board and the president. The covenant is based on a trust that there will be no surprises and that there will be appropriate and adequate consultation on major issues. Consultation does not mean obedience, but it does mean taking seriously the suggestions and objections of the faculty, whether expressed individually, at a full faculty or senate meeting, or by letter, and providing reasonable responses to their concerns.

Consulting with faculty on important decisions can help improve outcomes. I recall suggesting that a faculty member in business, who specialized in advertising and marketing, participate in the review of firms that responded to our request for proposals (RFP) for a new advertising campaign. The staff's initial response was to question why a faculty member was being included in the decision-making process. It took them some time to realize why it made sense: the professor had professional experience in the field and taught the subject to our students. I had a similar response when I included faculty members in deliberations about building construction and room design. My rationale was that form should follow philosophy (e.g., the design of a room should support the teaching and learning scheduled to take place in it), and experienced professors know the venue design that works best for different teaching styles.

While involving faculty in decisions can help, it may also cause some difficulties. I recall a time in New Jersey when the governor decided not to fund the state-negotiated salary and benefit increases for union members, which was the equivalent of a 9 percent cut—and the decision occurred in May! Our institution had to make major adjustments in a short period of time, and at a time when most faculty members were finished with their teaching duties. I appointed a special task force of faculty, staff, and key administrators to advise me on how to adjust expenses, expecting a serious exercise in setting priorities according to our strategic plan. Unfortunately, a strategic proposal did not happen. The faculty just could not bring themselves to agree on what should be eliminated and instead proposed a 10 percent cut across the board. I could not accept this and devised my own plan that I then reviewed with senior staff, faculty senate leadership, and the board. This example may help to illuminate the complexities for campus leadership when seeking faculty input on fiscal decisions.

Engaging with Students

For boards and presidents, the most important priority should be student success. Therefore, the board should know the goals for student retention from year to year and to graduation. They should know the goals for licensure exam results in the various professional fields of study and how financial aid policies, including those for merit aid through tuition discounting, support these goals. Are student clubs and teams as well as on-campus jobs supported as a strategic means for students to bond with others who support academic success?

Other questions relate to the adequacy of plans for controlling student indebtedness and federal financial aid default rates. How are admission standards set in order to achieve both the goals for diversity in the student body and for graduation rates for those who are admitted? In other words, who is responsible for the fit between admission standards and expectations for graduation when it comes to goals for student diversity, including economic diversity, legacy programs for the children of alumni and donors, and athletic or other "special talent" recruits?

A source of concern is the dismal record on graduation rates. Of 100 high school graduates, about 70 will graduate; 49 will enter college; and 25 will graduate with a four-year baccalaureate degree in six years.[19] Some of the delay in average graduation rates is due to cuts in state support for public institutions and a subsequent decline in the offering of courses needed to complete degree requirements on time. Another cause of delay is the number of hours many students have to work in order to pay for tuition, auto insurance, and other expenses. Another contributing factor is the lack of adequate preparation of students to pursue a degree. Boards should be aware of these issues related to student enrollment and success.

In some cases, students are included as members of the board of trustees. This is done usually with restrictions on attendance at executive sessions that are devoted to budget and personnel matters, and voting on certain matters. Student membership can lead to some interesting results.

Student involvement on the board caused some excitement at a state college in New Jersey, where students may elect a student trustee and a student trustee alternate. The student trustee may take part in all deliberations except executive sessions dealing with personnel and other confidential matters. A governor was attempting to install a state legislator as president by appointing trustees friendly to his sentiments. The vote for president resulted in a tie that was broken by the student trustee, who in open session voted against the proposed candidate. The newly appointed trustees were stunned by this action, as they had not anticipated the student vote.

While it may not be appropriate to include students as voting members on a board, including the president of the student government association and several representatives from the student body on the board's student life committee can be helpful. The board can also organize opportunities during lunch or dinner meetings to hear from students about special achievements and concerns.

Presidents should also meet with students both informally around campus and more formally at their governance meetings or in small groups gathered for breakfast, lunch, or dinner. The president should communicate student responses about what is going well on campus or what students wish to have included on the board agenda to the vice presidents or other related staff, as well as in his or her routine reports to the board. Students have a stake in the campus, and they too need to be heard.

Public Policy

At public institutions, local legislators, legislative committees, the governor's staff or appointment's counsel, the state secretary (or commissioner) of education, and the chair of the higher education governing or coordinating board are involved in campus leadership. Each constituent group has its own agenda, and each thinks it has a unique claim on the attention of university governance and leadership.

State government support is essential for public institutions, which have suffered cutbacks in state funding in recent years. Reductions have been made in base funding appropriations, capital budgets, student financial aid programs, and state-mandated expenses such as collective bargaining agreements. In some cases, state cuts can affect private institutions as well, especially in funds for student financial aid and capital bonding programs in which independent campuses participate. The role of the campus or system board in these cases is not only to monitor the strategic responses to reductions in revenue, but also to meet with and contact legislators about the importance of higher education in general and the necessity of state support in particular.

Board members should be aware of some unintended consequences to reductions in funding for public campuses. For example, reduced appropriations can result in reductions in faculty and course sections, resulting in less advising and course availability, causing students to spend more than four years to complete their undergraduate degree. This ends up costing the state and families more than anticipated.

Enrollment rates at public and private institutions change when state funding is cut and the economy is in decline at the same time. At such times, many families who might otherwise choose a private college will choose a public institution due to the tuition price differential and the attraction of honors programs for talented students. Since high school academic preparation and standardized test scores are highly correlated to family income, the increase in applications to state universities from more affluent families can lead to an increase in admissions competition for public institutions and reduce the number of students from less-well-off families who can meet the newly competitive standards.

Additional expenses can be incurred due to state government regulations, in particular those relating to teacher education programs. In New York State, for example, the regulations for the registration of programs such as music education change fairly often, and programs must be redesigned and registered. Such regulations may specify the particular credentials of those deemed qualified to teach and the number of credit hours they are allowed to teach, a requirement that can conflict with campus norms and collective bargaining agreements. Changes in these regulations can result in the expenditure of time and talent that could be better spent elsewhere, and can diminish a campus's competitive edge. This is especially true when so-called alternative pathways to teacher certification do not have the same requirements as university programs. State regulations require that new degree programs be approved by a state agency, thus slowing response time. In some cases, such as New York and New Jersey, the reviews for such approvals have been known to take years, thus reducing the flexibility of campuses to serve the public.

An institution's relationship with the community and local government can also have financial implications of which the board should be aware. For example, many communities impose a payment in lieu of taxes (PILOT) requirement on campuses. These charges, which are created to balance the lack of tax revenue from nonprofit (i.e., tax-exempt) institutions and reimburse the community for police and fire protection, can vary from a few tens of thousands of dollars to $1 million and more per year. In a well-known case, Princeton University entered a new PILOT settlement worth $18 million over the next ten years in addition to an existing $24 million payment.[20] The complaint was that the university benefited from its tax-exempt status to accumulate a massive endowment while the community's tax burden increased because the institution's operations and land were not being taxed. The possibilities of such charges and the uses to which they may be put are ample reason for the campus president and board chair to become well acquainted with local officials.

Examples of the effect of politicized public policy measures can be seen in the Texas "Breakthrough Solutions" of 2008, when the governor called for "7 Solutions"[21] to increase and measure institutional effectiveness, or in Kentucky, where courts have ruled to preserve the constitutional separation of powers protecting universities from intrusive practices by the legislative and executive branches of state government. In other examples, Governor Christine Todd Whitman of New Jersey decided in 1994 to do away with the Board of Higher Education and replace it with a commission. The Indiana Commission on Higher Education had been established at the same time and with essentially the same responsibilities as the New Jersey Department of Higher Education. However, in the previous twenty-seven years, the Indiana commission had issued no rules or regulations, while the New Jersey Department of Higher Education's rules and regulations covered over 500 pages of the administrative code. Yet the New Jersey department still did not fulfill its fundamental duties of state-wide planning and academic program review. The comparison reveals the effects of the different methods that may be taken in governance. The Indiana commission provided leadership through discussion and moral suasion, while the New Jersey department gave priority to power through regulation.

It is a good idea for the president and staff to become acquainted with state and federal legislators, as well as with state and federal financial aid programs. However, campus leaders should not become advocates for a policy that may be controversial or that might put the institution in the spotlight without first consulting with the board chair and perhaps the full board. A hard lesson can be learned from the example of a well-meaning campus president who filed an amicus brief on a controversial federal legal dispute without first checking with the board. As a result, both the president and the board chair were removed.

Regularly Assessing Board Performance, Policies, and Practices

The board should conduct an annual self-examination of its performance and an assessment of the board chair. Each board member and the president should complete the form. Members may attach suggestions about how the board could get higher ratings for any or all of the considerations. According to AGB, board assessment can help establish

- a clearer understanding of the board's primary roles and core responsibilities,
- a consensus on specific objectives and plans to improve board organization and performance,
- a better working relationship between the board and the chief executive,
- a renewed sense of commitment to the institution's mission and purpose,
- more productive board meetings, and
- a commitment to expectations for personal philanthropy.

The National Commission on College and University Board Governance defines "consequential" boards as those that meet the following tests:

- They improve value in their institutions and lead a restoration of public trust in higher education itself.
- They add value to institutional leadership and decision-making.
- They act to ensure the long-term sustainability of their institutions.
- They improve shared governance through attention to board-president relationships, re-invigoration of faculty shared governance, and leadership development for the board, the president, and faculty senate officers.
- They improve their own capacity and functionality.

- They focus their time on issues of greatest consequence.
- They hold themselves accountable for their own performance by modeling the behaviors and performance they expect of others.[22]

Therefore, the assessment of the board should consider these elements.

In order for boards to govern effectively, they must "think about how they acquire information, set policy, relate to other players, and assess outcomes. They cannot reasonably expect to find efficiency and agility in campus practices if they remain models of outdated practice."[23] The board should know all aspects of the institution, not just its finances and business operations. Fortunately, there are guides to assist boards in their duties. Two examples are *Evaluating the Board*, published by *Chief Executive* magazine, and *Presidents and Board Chairs: Navigating the Future Together*, published by the *Chronicle of Higher Education*.[24]

Moody's and Standard and Poor's are credit-rating agencies that evaluate the quality and effectiveness of board and executive leadership as well as of educational programs, financial management, and student outcomes. It is important for board members to know how their institution is rated, how it compares to others, and what is needed to improve its rating. Each campus meeting with bond-rating agency staff should include at least one trustee for both their wisdom and the potential "halo" effect. Campus governance is complicated because the challenges to higher education institutions are complicated, and they continue to evolve due to philosophical, legal, market, and political forces. Nevertheless, Moody's forecast is for stable seas if governance is strong and well grounded.

Campus Safety, Operations, and Maintenance

It is important for a board to review campus plans to deal with emergencies. Plans should be coordinated with the local community as well as with county and state emergency preparedness officials and other first responders. Because an emergency can occur at any time and without warning, campus officials should have good relations with local elected and appointed officials as well as with neighbors, especially as false alarms can occur frequently due to accidents, not by malicious intent alone.

Senior staff and others on campus should employ "table top" exercises to rehearse responses to simulated events such as hurricanes, fires, active shooter threats, and bomb scares. Campuses in the United States have had to deal with these and other emergencies, including earthquakes and flooding. With some states now permitting open carry laws that allow guns on campus and an increase in mental health concerns presented on campus by students and others, colleges must be prepared for the worst. Boards should be briefed periodically on how well prepared the campus is for such events, especially whether the campus security force is armed. In a similar vein, campuses must be prepared for disruptions to cyber security and plan for how campus operations will continue in the case of an emergency.

Chapter 3

Board Membership

Who Is on the Board?

Boards should ensure that they include members who understand the purposes of higher education and the mission of the institution, the markets for students, and the challenges and competitive advantage of the university they hold in trust, people who have the gumption to ask questions about things they do not understand or with which they disagree. Members should not seek the position for prestige any more than a corporate director should need his or her position because of the stipend. They should be invested in terms of voluntary donations or stock ownership. In both cases, board members must collectively have the expertise necessary to guide a complex organization with multiple functions and sources of revenue. Board service is an opportunity for learning, judgment, and setting institutional direction in fulfillment of historic missions and state priorities. It is not simply a resume builder. Effective trusteeship requires time, talent, and treasure. It is not something to enhance an obituary.

Board members may wish to serve because they believe it is time to give back to an institution that was important to them at a critical time in their lives. While this motive is honorable, it does not reflect the true nature of what is needed for the position. Board service, if done well, is work, and it takes energy, imagination, and commitment—not old sentiments revisited. Board members should know the positive reasons they serve and understand what is rewarding and challenging about serving. They should know how the board chair and president can help them be more effective in their roles on the board. Board members help frame the issues; in this way the board not only governs but also leads.

The increasing demands on governance have made it necessary for university board members to be knowledgeable about the purposes and history of higher education at large as well as of the institutions they serve, just as corporations and special agencies need board members who are knowledgeable about products, technology, or services; the industry in which their organization competes; and the markets to be served. This is why it is useful to have senior academics from another, noncompeting institution on a university board.

Previous experience in higher education is often undervalued when it comes to board membership. As stated earlier, corporate boards and some public utilities have been criticized for not including members who know the business, the market, and the competition. Similarly, college and university boards often lack members with professional experience in the field of higher education. This is important to consider, as what may work well on banking, manufacturing, or entertainment boards may not work well in higher education. University trustees need to know about the complexities of higher education financing, quality controls, government regulations, competition, tuition and financial aid policies, international student recruitment, and so on if they are to be effective in their role.

There are an average of twelve trustees per public institution, and twenty-nine per independent institution. The average for affiliated foundation boards, which operate mostly as fundraising arms of public colleges and universities, is thirty-one. If one multiplies those averages by the number of institutions, it is estimated that there are some 80,000 college and university trustees in the United States. Women make up 32 percent of board members, an increase from 12 percent in 1969. Racial and ethnic minorities account for 17 percent of trustees at public institutions and 11.1 percent at independent colleges. Two-thirds of trustees are between the ages of fifty and sixty-nine, and more than 75 percent of trustees at public and private institutions are either active in business or a professional service practice like accounting or law, or retired from these fields. Only 7.4 percent of members are or were faculty or administrators in higher education.[1]

There are many types of trustees, with a range of professional experience and personality styles. These differences can affect how the board operates, as well as relations with the president. Board effectiveness is enhanced by a diverse membership. In addition to diversity in terms of ethnicity and race, which are important in order to reflect these dimensions of diversity among the students and communities served, board members should also be diverse in terms of professional backgrounds, age, and economic status. Such diversity is more likely than homogeneity to contribute to robust discussions about the mission, direction, challenges, and accomplishments of the institution. Some board members may be fraternity brothers or sorority sisters, classmates, or neighbors in the same community. They need to be careful that their social discussions do not become mini-board meetings with conclusions that leave other board members out of the loop.

When discussing the composition of boards and committees, the notion of diversity is sometimes misunderstood. It is not simply a celebration of variety for its own sake or intended as part of an effort to overcome past patterns of discrimination. The salutary benefits of diversity (i.e., intentionally seeking out and drawing on diverse backgrounds, experiences, and points of view) are well known and have been empirically demonstrated as beneficial to problem identification and the quality of decision-making. However, a goal for diversity on the board should not ignore the requirement for relevant competence. No one should be a symbol; all should be elected because they can contribute substantively, even if not financially.

Helpful and Unhelpful Board Members

In my years as a university president, I have known board members who were especially helpful and those who were not. I recall those who were wise and always came prepared, even if their jobs required extensive international travel, while others arrived unprepared but were argumentative and intrusive anyway. Some were domineering in board discussions, without giving others a chance to talk, while others followed the herd, even though they had a voice and a vote equal to others. Still another trustee type is the one who seems more interested in becoming the board chair than in helping the board and the president govern and manage effectively.

Board members do not have to be all knowing. It is perfectly fine for a board member to say, "Please repeat that. I do not understand." When board members say this, they inevitably find others who confess that they did not understand either. I have known board members who asked helpful questions in a manner that was probing but not aggressive, while others recommended changes and prescribed actions without fully understanding the issue at hand.

The most effective board members bring questions, not prescriptions. There are board members, and others, who insist on a course of action because they heard or read that another institution or organization acted in a particular way. I recall a board member who told the assembled trustees and senior staff that the university brand statement was too general. When I asked him about the brand statement for his company, he exclaimed that they were having the same problem and that no one at his firm agreed with him about it. So, he was telling us to do something that his own corporate colleagues could not do to his satisfaction. It would have been better for him to pose a question about the brand statements of competing universities and ask how we specified our competitive strengths.

On another occasion, I interviewed a trustee who had proposed that his institution cut its tuition because another had gained front-page coverage in a major newspaper and extensive reporting on national radio for doing so. A fellow trustee, an academic from another university, asked whether the board was aware of the competitive setting of that university and the size of its endowment. It turned out that the financial and competitive circumstances of the institutions were dramatically different, with the private college covered in the news having a substantial endowment and numerous public university competitors nearby. The net tuition of the university whose trustee introduced the topic was already nearly 20 percent lower than the tuition at the university covered in the media, with a much smaller endowment. The trustee withdrew his prescription reluctantly.

Imagine, though, if instead of proposing an action, the first trustee had asked about his institution's tuition level relative to the competitive environment and inquired whether his institution's tuition was higher, lower, or the same as competing campuses. This question, then, could have led to a discussion of pricing strategy relative to the needs and competitive position of the institution for which he had a fiduciary responsibility.

This "prescription versus question" conflict is not unique to my own experience. John Lombardi, former president of the University of Florida, describes an enthusiastic trustee who expressed concern that his university was not "keeping up." When asked what he meant, the trustee referred to big data, crowd sourcing, the cloud, MOOCs, and other technological advances he considered as tipping points in a period of dynamic, disruptive change. The trustee wanted his university to take specific actions quickly. Rather than asking what the university was doing about these and other innovations, this trustee was recommending actions that, at the time, were expensive, were largely untested, and would take funds away from agreed-upon goals and objectives.

It is most helpful to have board members who ask questions and who are aware of comparable governance decisions at other institutions. For example, on one occasion a trustee proposed tying the compensation of the president and vice presidents to a set of measurable metrics. In this case, a trustee who was a university professor elsewhere reminded her fellow trustees of the scandal over presidential compensation at their institution some years earlier that had resulted in a settlement agreement with the IRS. She suggested that it would not be a good idea to have an unusual compensation plan, and others agreed.

Of course, having prior experience in higher education board service does not always mean the trustee will agree with campus leadership. This is particularly true in the case of trustees accustomed to meeting only a financial bottom line. For example, a businessman who serves as a trustee of two (noncompeting) universities complained to me about the costs of tenure. I acknowledged that tenure is equivalent to a capital cost, but explained that the issue of cost he was citing had nothing to do with tenure. He was commenting on the number of full-time faculty and why colleges always seemed to want to add more. My response was to explain that full-time faculty members are more likely to be available to students for individual and group advising, and more likely to involve students in their research. Full-time faculty also are responsible for maintaining the quality of the curriculum and keeping it up to date, hiring and nurturing new faculty, and ensuring that the faculty hired are able to maintain the quality and integrity of the program. Furthermore, I said that the protections provided by academic freedom inherent in tenure are needed by part-time faculty as well. They, too, deserve protection from criticism by those who are unqualified but may disagree anyway with certain research pursuits and testable theories. Nevertheless, it is true that tenure is under review in a de facto way, as the percentage of contingent or part-time faculty grows and the average age of currently tenured faculty rises.

Board members should be aware of the consequences of certain behaviors. I recall a trustee who could become belligerent if he did not get his way, others who seemed to fawn over the chairperson, and still others who would not say a word until after the board meeting, when they would call to complain about the chair. I have experienced trustees who could not ask a question without sounding like skeptics, and another who was often seen whispering to fellow board members. Once, when I noticed this, I approached him and heard him say, "They are eating our lunch." When I asked what he meant, he identified one of our competitors. I asked, "Why didn't you tell me what you have heard in the community instead of leaving me in the dark?" Unhelpful negativity is of no benefit to the board or the institution at large.

In one interview, I spoke to a board member about his service on a university board and asked why he decided to resign. After three incidents in which he found the president to be violating this trustee's sense of good judgment, it was the chairman's proposal that persuaded him to leave the board. At a meeting, the chair told the assembled members that it was time to adjust the president's compensation and asked for a motion of approval. The person I interviewed said that he asked if the board would discuss the president's performance and the amount of increase recommended. The chair's reply was that if the trustee needed such information, they could talk after the meeting. Feeling that his questions were not being respected, the trustee resigned. This is obviously not how to encourage board engagement or to fulfill the responsibilities of a board.

Lack of clear and honest communication can be as frustrating for the president as it is for board members. I recall a time when I had concluded that we had to eliminate football rather than academic programs and faculty in response to severe state budget cutbacks. I discussed this action with the board on three separate occasions over several months and had unanimous agreement from them. The agreement was unanimous, that is, until I announced the decision. Then, two board members criticized my action—until the board chair intervened and reminded them and the other board members of the meetings during which we had discussed this plan and they had agreed to the action.

Even well-intentioned board members must be aware of potential conflicts. In one instance, I was obligated to ask the board chair to talk to a trustee who had been active on campus for years before being elected to the board and did not want to give up her prior relationships. She had taught in a unit and donated sufficient funds to have the unit's home building named in her husband's honor. She did not seem to realize the complications she was causing for the dean and provost by her socializing and familiarity with the staff.

In another example, a university president told me of a time when a board member, who was a real estate developer, wanted to take advantage of the governor's proposal to use college and university property for business developments that would increase employment in the region. The president had concerns about the legal and political implications of the proposal, especially since the developer was a donor to the college and would reap significant financial and political benefits from participation in the new state program. The president sought the opinion of an attorney, who in turn wrote a letter advising that participation in this project was not a good idea. The trustee was not happy, but the university avoided a conflict of interest and potential public embarrassment. In fact, a major scandal did result at another campus in a different part of the state over the same issue. Unfortunately, while a conflict of interest was avoided, the relationship between the president and the board member was put in jeopardy.

Helpful trustees bring a clear head to deliberations. I am especially fond of a trustee who, when considering whether we should hire a firm to install an energy management system at its expense and receive half of the savings, pointed out that we did not need the vendor to do this. The trustee explained that we could afford to install the energy management system ourselves, pay up front, and keep all the savings. We had experienced several years of state budget cuts and had been conserving money, but the trustee convinced us not to "think poor." It is a move like this that makes a trustee valuable.

On yet another occasion, while considering a tuition increase, a board member changed the tone and texture of a discussion that had become tense with arguments for either no change or a minimal change in the tuition rate. This board member said, essentially, "We will not make progress by cutting our revenue or charging less than we are worth. If we believe what we say about the quality of education here, we should price our tuition accordingly." He was not suggesting that we ignore the philosophical, political, and market influences at work, but that we approach the setting of tuition with a more thoughtful rationale.

The most valuable trustees fulfill their duties with caring and imagination. One such trustee helped the campus deal with a student petition demanding that the college allow fraternities to start on campus. Some trustees were adamantly opposed to approving fraternities because of their national reputation for excessive drinking and sexual assault, but our attorney said that, as a public institution, we could not ban them on the basis of what we thought they might do. A trustee helped us frame the discussion so that it was not "for" or "against" fraternities, but rather focused on what needs the students thought fraternities would meet. That is, what was the question to which fraternities were the answer? With this approach, the board and president were able to guide the development of a social service fraternity and sorority system that became an important influence on student satisfaction, success, retention, and graduation rates.

Other trustees can be helpful with neighbor and civic relations because of their standing in the community. Others serve as a kind of moral compass when it comes to taking the goal of diversity seriously. Still others act as representatives of the institution's history and serve as cheerleaders for its founding values.

I have heard many other stories about board members who served their institutions well, even by saying something as simple as "If it's not broke, why fix it?" to fellow board members who were advocating a particular argument. This is essentially a conservative approach to board oversight and may work well to protect the university of the future from the actions of the present, a primary responsibility of the board.

With so many different personality types, it is important for board members to socialize and get to know each other as whole people, not just as board members with philosophical positions. It is through social functions and informal conversations that members can develop the trust necessary for each to express honest opinions openly and ask questions during the business of the board.

Nominating a Board Chair and Officers

As Brian Mitchell said, "Just as presidents must have the courage to manage and lead, board chairs must have the skills and courage to preside."[2] When deciding on a candidate for chair of the board, it is important to consider leadership qualities, including the ability to engage all members in the work of the board. An effective chair must have emotional intelligence and empathy, assuring that all voices have a chance to be heard. He or she also has to have the ability to handle topics and suggestions offered that are not relevant to the current discussion. Delegation of such a matter to a committee or to a later meeting may be in order.

The chair must also be able effectively to manage minority factions within the board. Often, however, board leadership roles are awarded to the most generous donors, even if generosity is not highly correlated with good leadership qualities.

According to AGB, an effective board chair

- makes certain that the institution has an agreed-upon vision of what it aspires to be and that there is board support for the vision;
- understands that a respectful, productive relationship is central to success;
- builds strong relationships with other key players, including fellow board members, the president, administration, faculty, students, and alumni;
- forges consensus among those key constituents; and
- understands the dimensions of the board chair's power within the institution's model of shared governance—the relationship among the governing board, president, and faculty—and understands the points of leverage to get things done.

It is certainly important for the board chair to be in a position to encourage others to be generous. If the role of the chair in fundraising is deemed to be essential, then one might consider how the roles of chair and vice chair can work together. In fact, the best leadership is a team approach involving the chair, the vice chair, the secretary, and the president. More minds at work on a problem can be better than one, and the president is better served by having close working relationships with multiple board members rather than with just one.

The advice of the president is helpful in these selections, but asking for it can put him or her in an awkward position. I recall being asked by the board chair for my opinion about the person he wanted to succeed him as chair, and I hesitated. I said that a president should not be opining on who should be chair because his or her honesty could lead to difficult relations with either the current or the next chair. After all, the president works for the board and should not be put in the position of determining who should be the chair. In addition, the president should not be put in the position of asking a member to leave the board or to change his or her behavior in board meetings. Yet I was put in all three positions.

When the trustee affairs committee concludes that a board member should not be re-elected when his or her term is up, it should be the board chair, or the chair of the committee, not the president, who calls with the news. This approach may avoid potential conflict and protect the president from being in an uncomfortable and untenable position

It is important to have a board chair who can lead the disparate members in productive discussions. This does not mean that the person is selfless, but it does mean that he or she puts the operations of the board above personal interests or "hobby horses." No individual other than the chair or another designated person should speak for the board. Disputes about decisions should stay in the boardroom. If a member cannot follow this rule, he or she should leave the board, while still maintaining the duty of obedience to the charter and loyalty to the institution. Finally, according to *Board Forward*, "the goal of the board chair is to ensure the participation of board members and facilitate productive discussions that drive the organization forward."[3]

Board Terms

For board officers, it is a good practice to limit terms to one year each, with the expectation that, if all goes well, officers will be re-elected each year for a total of three years. While practices vary, one person should not serve as chair for longer than three years unless there are unusual circumstances. The board should have others ready to serve in leadership roles. If the trustee affairs committee is doing its job of selecting new board members, orienting both new and continuing board members, rotating membership on committees, and providing continuing education and leadership opportunities for members, there should be a roster of potential candidates for officer posts. Boards should have a process for trustee development, so that there is always leadership talent available,

When nominating a candidate to the full board, the trustee affairs committee should indicate the person's term. Ninety percent of boards specify the length of a single term, which, on average, is 5.8 years for public institutions and 3.6 years for independent campuses. Public boards meet an average of 7.4 times per year, while independent institution boards meet, on average, three to four times per year.[4]

Many boards have as an ideal that one-third of the board should be up for re-election each year, with each member elected for a three-year term. A good practical guide is to limit members to twelve years in total, or four three-year terms. (Some boards prefer three three-year terms, for a total of nine years.) While it is at times tempting to want someone to stay on the board longer, it is usually better to have them leave the board for at least a year. Then, if the board and the former member want to start again, they can.

The number of terms should depend upon the institution and its needs and challenges, but the board should not harm itself by sticking to a rule that could diminish its capacity. Beware of certitudes and consider them cautiously.

Identifying Candidates for the Board

What are the best ways to identify, vet, and orient potential board members? At independent colleges and universities, the president and members of the fundraising staff customarily review the names of active and accomplished alumni and friends of the college or university to consider who might be good candidates. Board membership should be a coveted position, earned by service and a commitment to assist in the fulfillment of the campus mission through good governance. The process for vetting board members will be different for public and private institutions and may vary considerably among individual universities.

Some campuses use executive search firms to find board members. When making this decision, campus leaders should consider whether student tuition revenue should be used to pay for finding a trustee. There often are highly accomplished alumni willing to come to campus to speak to and mentor students at their places of work. These visits can be "tryouts" for a larger role. Leaders should search first among the alumni and friends of the university when seeking board candidates.

While philanthropy must be a high priority, it should not be the only one. Board membership should not be two-tiered, with one set of members to do the work of governance and another set included for their capacity as donors. For institutions that favor this approach, a better model to follow is that used by most public colleges and universities. In these cases, the university has both a governing board and a separate foundation board whose mission is to raise both funds and the public profile of the institution.

It may be tempting to try out a potential board member by asking him or her to serve as a nontrustee member of a committee. This may cause potential friction should the board member ask, as time goes by, why they are serving on a board committee but have not yet been selected to be a member of the board. A better route may be to ask the person to work on a special ad hoc task force with a limited term focused on some strategic issue such as tuition planning. Such involvement will not only test the candidate's degree of interest and expertise, but also provide an opportunity to see how they relate to others and their degree of tact, as well as to learn whether they have a personal agenda that might be disruptive to board deliberations. The assignment can also provide an extended orientation to the board for the person selected. Avenues such as academic unit advisory boards or the alumni association board should be pursued if the goal is to engage potential donors in the life of the university. Membership on the board of trustees usually should not be the first step.

In my two presidencies, I appointed advisory councils of accomplished people in different professional fields to whom I could turn for advice. The groups would meet several times per year and discuss pressing issues, such as strategic plans, new programs, bond-rating agency presentations, and proposals for facilities, among other topics. While the intention was to have an advisory body separate from the governing board, as a kind of "rehearsal" board, several members did become trustees and served well. They were committed, informed, insightful, and vetted.

It is not only advisable that candidates have some board experience, unless he or she is a candidate for a "young alumni" category, but also it is important that they have experience with best practices in board governance. Bad habits from a for-profit or not-for-profit organization, where "old boy" networks might prevail, may affect the performance of the person on a university board.

Those who are identified as potential candidates should then be evaluated in relation to board needs by referring to a matrix listing the names of current board members on the vertical axis and the areas of expertise desired on the board across the horizontal axis. Board members' professional experiences should reflect the diversity of the college's academic offerings, and, ideally, its membership should reflect the diversity in terms of demographic characteristics. The matrix is then analyzed to determine the areas of expertise, including higher education, fields of accomplishment, and personal characteristics, that are lacking and desired. The resulting empty cells are then used as guides to find suitable alumni and friends to be invited for follow-up interviews by the board's nominating committee or another small group of trustees.

The processes at public colleges and universities may vary if the governor or the legislature has authority over the appointment of trustees. In these cases, the institution might suggest names of particularly experienced and valued people for review by the governor's appointments counsel, or the governor's staff might simply announce new board member appointments. The final choice in any case will often be made on political grounds, perhaps even requiring the approval of the state senator in the district within which the college is located. (One hopes that this senator will not hold up the appointment as a trade-off with another senator whose vote is wanted on an entirely different matter.) Further recommendations for this process may be found in Callan and Honetschlager's recommendations for improving trustee selection in the public sector.[5]

The trustee affairs committee is the body to contemplate the composition of the board and its officers, and to make recommendations to the full board. The president usually serves on this and all committees, except the audit committee, in an ex officio role. The president and other institutional officers may be invited to audit committee meetings but may not be a member.

For those who meet the criteria for membership set by the board, the president will propose to the board's trustee affairs committee that the candidate's credentials be reviewed by the committee and, if agreed upon, interviewed. Following the interview, the committee will discuss whether the candidate is ready for board membership and, if the answer is "yes," confirm the person's interest and forward a recommendation to the committee and then to the full board.

Conducting Interviews

Once potential board members have been identified, the president and staff will want to meet with the prospects individually; learn more about them, including their experience on other boards; tell them about any pressing issues at the institution so they are not surprised later on; and, if they are not already active on campus, ask them to be involved in some activity such as the ad hoc task forces mentioned previously.

While this process can result in an awkward situation when it is decided that a candidate is not a good fit, perhaps because of a conflict of interest or a lack of experience, it is more often than not an effective process. It is certainly important to the long-term interests of the institution.

I recall once during an interview when an enthusiastic trustee told the candidate that he would be an excellent member, but said this before consulting with the other trustees taking part in the meeting. They were not as enthusiastic and an excuse about timing was offered to back out of the apparent invitation to board service. Another example is telling. We interviewed an active alumna who was head of an art museum founded in memory of a world-renowned artist couple. As the campus had robust art programs, enrollment, and exhibits, we thought she would be a great addition. Unfortunately for us, during the interview we learned that she solicited funds for private gifts from some of the same sources we did. Some board members became concerned about this potential conflict of interest and competition. In the end, we decided not to offer a board seat to an alumna whom we liked and respected a great deal. This may have been our loss.

During the interview with the prospective trustee, the president and board members should talk about the board's philosophy, operations, and expectations. This is the time when informal conversations about the institution and its governance can take place. In preparation for the interview, the candidate should be given the bylaws, information about the organization of the board, the strategic plan, the budget, and other pertinent information.

The board members should already have analyzed the candidate's resume and degree of involvement on the campus and in board service elsewhere. They also should have a clear idea of how the candidate could add to the board's strengths. Is it in terms of professional expertise, experience in governance, or some other desired attribute?

Board members should discuss the candidate's degree of interest, preparation for the meeting as well as for board service, level of experience in and approach to serving as a board member, any potential conflicts of interest in terms of commitments of time or resources, and any concerns he or she might have about the university or board service. This is the time to assess the level of knowledge and experience beyond the candidate's area of expertise and to determine their overall leadership qualities.

If the trustees who interviewed the candidate decide to forward a recommendation of election to the full board, and if the candidate is still interested in service, the next step is clear. If the board chair is to meet every candidate, as is sometimes the case, and if the chair was not part of the interview party, then another meeting must be scheduled.

Upon making the nomination, the board must decide whether the candidate should attend the meeting at which a vote on his or her status will be taken. If there has been sufficient communication about the candidate between the board chair and the board, it is usually satisfactory to have the candidate come to the board meeting, remain outside the room while the vote is taken, and then be brought in to meet the remainder of the board. The candidate should be given a roster of trustees that includes brief biographical statements and photographs so that he or she can identify individuals at the meeting.

Once elected, the new trustee should participate in orientation sessions organized by the board administrator and attended by the president, the vice presidents, and perhaps another trustee. Some boards have trustee mentors for new board members. The mentor takes the time to help in orientation to board service and in introducing the new member to fellow board members on board days and on other occasions.

Orientation

A single orientation session is not sufficient. Boards should think of the first session as Orientation 101, to be followed systematically with 201, 301, and so on. (See Appendix B for a guide to information that should be included in the orientation packet.)

Some states have mandated orientation sessions for new trustees of public institutions and have even developed official certifications for successful completion of the training. Texas offers online tutorials for trustees, and Oklahoma developed a model for training after prompting by the legislature. In some cases, the impetus for developing training sessions for public university trustees followed controversies regarding board governance. This can occur when the board departs from its role and tries to substitute itself or its chairperson for strong and effective presidential leadership.

Through proper orientation, the board should be able to avoid controversy. Orientation is a time for board members to learn more about their responsibilities. The board's role is to consider decisions in terms of institutional strategy, priorities, and risk. Members must be appropriately prepared before making these decisions. A botched process in reaching a negative decision can have both legal and political consequences.

In preparation for the orientation session, the new trustee should be given a packet of materials that includes information about the history, mission, bylaws (see a sample in Appendix C), organizational processes, finances, duties and expectations for board members, and more. These orientation discussions should cover the whole of the institution's mission, including the mission for teaching and advising in relation to research, scholarship, and other creative activities of the faculty. The members should also be reminded of the range of students on campus, as it may be too easy for a board dominated by alumni with baccalaureate degrees to focus their attention on traditional undergraduates and ignore returning adults, master's degree candidates, and doctoral and postdoctoral students.

The orientation should include a meeting with the leaders of the faculty senate and an introduction to the idea of shared governance and how it works in practice. This discussion should include an overview of how the faculty senate is organized and spends its time, what proportion of faculty participate in electing the members, how it fulfills its responsibilities for the curriculum and academic quality, and what challenges it faces. If there is a faculty union, the new trustee should be guided through the collective bargaining agreement (CBA) and the distinction between shared governance that involves the faculty senate and the CBA (which includes the faculty union as a signatory), which is focused solely on compensation and working conditions. A tour of the campus and all facilities is an important part of any orientation and good preparation for future deliberations. For institutions with multiple locations, the tour will take place over several visits.

As a creative twist, the president might ask the head of the theater department to lead a tour of the campus and comment on it as a stage set, with an eye toward lines of sight, landscaping, and the aesthetics of the scene. The campus grounds, after all, should support the "story line" of the institution's mission to inspire the people and care for the environment of the campus. (Following the tour, the board or president might outline notes for discussion with the staff responsible for buildings and grounds and discuss any needed changes. For example, when discussing the design of a new building or plans for a complete renovation of a building, it is important to consider where food service can be located and where paintings and works of sculpture can be displayed. The facility may be designed as a home for the nursing program or for general classrooms, but at some point it may be used for events where food service would be desirable. All buildings should include spaces for art displays intended to soothe, inspire, and provoke conversations as well as to honor student, faculty, and alumni achievements.)

New and continuing trustees should not enter an orientation program as passive vessels. Prospective, new, and continuing board members should ask questions such as the following of the board chair and president:

- What are the institution's goals? What are the impediments to achieving these goals?
- What is the president's philosophy of leadership?
- What are the criteria for selecting the institutions used for comparisons in terms of goals and achievements?
- What is the president's philosophy and approach to strategic planning?
- Why was I selected as a board member? What do you expect of me? What are my basic duties?
- What does the president worry about when he or she is alone and thinking about the institution?
- Why do we think that our business or economic model is sustainable for the long term?
- What are the limitations to my talking with faculty, senior staff, other staff, and students while serving on the board?
- May I answer questions about the campus when posed by the media?
- What is the approach to engaging consultants? What types are used?
- What forms of collaboration does the institution have with other institutions and organizations?
- What are the plans for succession of the board, board officers, and the executive team?
- What are the internal and external forms of quality control, such as routine academic program and administrative unit reviews and accreditation visits?
- What are the most common ethical and legal challenges faced by the board?

- How do criticisms of higher education nationally relate to our campus?
- How does this board balance governance with management and avoid micromanagement?
- Have any board members in recent years resigned, and for what reasons?
- How does the board define diversity in its membership, and how well does it achieve it?
- What was the biggest challenge faced by the board in recent years, and how did it manage it?

These and other questions can prompt productive discussions about the institution and its governance, and about the role and expectations of the trustee. A central part of the discussion should be about what it will take to help the institution continue to improve, with attention to the institution's goals, the reason for these goals, and the requirements for success in achieving them.

Chapter 4

Processes and Procedures

Board Meetings

Boards typically meet four times per year, usually for one and a half or two days each time. Special meetings can always be scheduled when needed. After each meeting, the president should meet with the chair and, if available, the other officers, to debrief the meeting and discuss items for follow up before the next meeting. The president should then draft a memorandum with this summary for discussion with the senior staff and the board administrator. This summary will help in preparing the next agenda (see Appendix D for a sample board meeting agenda).

At each meeting, the board should hold an executive session in two parts. In the first part, the president can discuss confidential items with the board, perhaps elaborating on some topics noted in a report sent in advance. The president prepares the report to the board using a standard format to comment on board business, board member involvement on campus, and other important topics (see Appendix E for a sample confidential periodic report of the president). This confidential report is to be read by the board only and may include the following:

- Current campus issues of particular interest
- Summaries of the topics for each committee agenda at the upcoming meeting, especially those deserving special attention
- Leadership development initiatives underway for vice presidents, deans, and others such as the board administrator
- Administrative and financial matters, including operations audits and comments on any reports to the faculty senate
- Alumni and fundraising activities and results, including travel plans and new gifts
- Local community, state, and federal issues affecting the campus in particular and higher education at large
- Highlights of student, faculty, and staff accomplishments on and off campus
- Comments about the president's recent, current, or projected professional activities on behalf of the university

After the first part of the executive session, the president should leave while the board continues to discuss personnel, legal issues, and other confidential matters, including the president's performance and contract. It should be noted that public university and college boards operate under so-called sunshine laws and are restricted as to the topics to be discussed in executive session and how they must be reported on when in public session.

An alternative to organizing the board's deliberations around committee agendas that are aligned with the institution's administrative functions is to organize the work around mission-specific priorities, such as the overarching goals of the strategic plan. Still another alternative is to have a combination of both. For example, committees would still meet in regular format for a period of time but then the members of the committees would reassemble in separate sessions focusing on particular goals. These could include such topics as student retention, healthcare programming, regional competition, online programs, research funding, or alumni participation. Then, the full board would meet as a whole and not only hear reports from the standing committees but also from the separate sessions before engaging in discussion and decision-making.

While it may seem like a small detail, an important consideration for each meeting is the location and seating format. For maximum participation, board members should be comfortable both in their seats and at the table. They should be able to see each other's facial expressions as well as hear each other. If there are PowerPoint presentations or other visual materials, all members must be able to see them without moving. While teleconference meetings can work well for a single topic, or perhaps two, they do not make for effective meetings of the full board, unless it is an unusually small board. With two dozen or more members and a set of complex topics, members should meet in person. Background noises such as a dog barking or the clatter of dishes can be unnecessary distractions.

Rather than distributing materials at a meeting, it is more helpful to send an organized packet of information needed at least one week in advance. In addition to mailing material in advance, many boards use an internet or intranet portal to post not only information for the upcoming meeting, but also past agendas and meeting minutes as well as basic documents. These include bylaws, strategic plans, the calendar for decision-making during the year, and brief biographical statements and photographs of board members, vice presidents, deans, and board administrator.

The quantity of materials to be prepared for each meeting of the full board and committees is a subject of some debate. The president should provide as much information as necessary, and individual board members can decide what to study and what to skim. Preparation for a board meeting can be time consuming, including the preparation of documents for decisions, staff and committee discussions of a topic for a future decision, and the compilation of general information thought to be of relevance to the board. It does take a lot of work if done properly, and the discipline of having board meetings on specific days and at specific times adds pressure to prepare the materials in a timely way. However, preparing this information can be good discipline even if the board does not meet, as it helps to prepare the president or other parties to address potential questions from trustees.

Preparations for meetings can be enhanced by a conference call with the president, board officers, committee chairs, and the board administrator several weeks before the meeting date. During this call, the group can discuss the topics and the background material needed for a robust and helpful deliberation of items for discussion and action. Then, the vice presidents should prepare committee agenda items according to a standard format. After the president reviews and finalizes the agendas for the committees and full board, the board administrator should prepare the agenda books, post the materials on the board portal, and prepare the materials for mailing.

It is essential to have the right information, well organized, easy to read, and as complete as possible, in order for the board to have a thorough discussion before an action is taken at the meeting or prepared for action at the next meeting. It is often important to have a full discussion of the proposed action, alternatives, and implications at one meeting and then put the items on the agenda for decision at the next meeting.

To help organize these discussions, each board needs an astute, intelligent, careful listener as the board administrator. As noted in an Association of Governing Boards of Universities and Colleges (AGB) publication, the essential characteristics for a board administrator are "competence, character, courage, and credibility." Board administrators must be not only meeting planners and minutes scribes, but also the link between the president and the board. As such, they can be put in a position of mixed loyalties, wanting and needing to be a member of the institutional team, but also finding that they are in a position to hear negative comments about the president or asked probing questions about the administration. Diplomacy is key.[1]

Typically, a board receives three types of documents: decisions to be made, discussion only (whether as preparation for a future decision or for more general educational purposes), and information.

- *Decision*: Items should include background information to put the decision in context, alternative courses of action considered, and an assessment of the pros and cons of each alternative. Then the recommendation and its probable implications should be articulated. Finally, attachments should be included that provide more background information as well as a resolution to be voted on by the board and, if approved by the board, signed by the secretary.
- *Discussion*: Just as the template for decision items can give the board a quick overview of a proposed decision and its implications, the template for discussion items can help the board understand the item and its importance. In this case, the sections are: (1) background, including why this topic is important to discuss; (2) considerations, including how one might think about this topic; (3) next steps, including what might be proposed in the future; and (4) attachments, including the document to be discussed and any supplementary or additional explanatory material.
- *Information*: Items are not proposed for action and do not necessarily require discussion, but include information that the president or board leaders think should be made known to the board. In this case, the template includes the topic (i.e., the relevance of the information to board governance, higher education in general, or institutional strategic planning in particular), the priority for the item, and any attachments.

One of the discussion items at each meeting could be a report by a dean of an academic unit or director of an administrative unit (See Appendix F for a template for the dean's report). The dean or director's report to the board gives the board members an opportunity for an in-depth discussion about the substance of one important component of the institution and the person who leads it. This is timely to schedule when the board is considering a new academic program, a facilities project, campus safety, or an update to an academic program review. The reports should be prepared in advance and sent to the board with the other agenda materials. At the meeting, the dean or director can give an overview of national trends; national or regional competition; student, faculty, and staff accomplishments; the comparative advantages and disadvantages of the program; and goals and opportunities as related to the campus mission.

Through designated meetings and readings, both new and continuing trustees can learn about national issues, such as the federal government's college scorecard initiative intended to provide prospective students and their families more complete information about average annual costs, academic offerings, and retention and graduation rates, as well as projected personal income. Trustees should also learn about ethical issues related to domestic and international student recruitment as well as those related to the reporting of data to various agencies and publications. Some institutions, after all, have been known to present flattering but inaccurate information to such sources.

The university or college president will probably talk with the board chair about once per week, or more often when necessary. These regular talks may help to ensure a policy of "no surprises" so that broader board involvement is used only when necessary. Nevertheless, the president and board chair should also be prepared for the possibility of new issues.

No surprises! This is an essential truth in the relationship between a president and the board, and vice versa. Board members are not bystanders, but fundamental partners with the president for the effective accomplishment of goals. However, it is also true that boards should not be told too much too soon; for example, early signals about a drop in admission deposits might lead to overreaction. Timing is essential. No surprises, for sure, but no undue panic either. Judgment is required in board communications as in all other matters.

To keep the board up to date on faculty concerns, the provost and president should meet monthly with faculty senate officers. With specific regard to labor issues, the president should invite the president of the faculty collective bargaining unit to meet for coffee two or three times a year. Even if there are no immediate issues of concern, these meetings can make clear that communication lines are always open. Inevitably, an issue will come up during a meeting that can be addressed.

The president should also meet regularly with the president of the student government association (SGA) and meet with the full SGA senate two to three times per year to give an update and ask for comments. Other valuable meetings may include the editor of the student newspaper and the leaders of the campus radio or television stations. They represent important voices on campus and should be informed about campus developments. A president can learn from their concerns, and it is best that they, too, not be surprised.

Following any unusual occurrence, whether a protest by students, a building take-over, a strike by clerical workers, or police or fire department presence on your campus or another, the president should hold a special meeting of key staff and perhaps faculty. Valuable questions to get the discussion started include

- What can we learn from this?
- What did we (or they) do right?
- What could we (or they) have done better?

The questions may seem rhetorical, but they are not. While a few staff may say that there is nothing to learn from complaints, often these questions will lead to valuable outcomes. Students do not protest gratuitously; unions do not go on strike without reason. There usually is an explanation. Reasons can include the perceived failure of the university to provide the faculty and courses promised, unannounced changes in financial aid policy, silence by the campus administration in the face of an act of violence, or failure to reply to a letter of complaint about a topic deemed serious by members of the community. Protests at Yale, Princeton, Harvard, Oxford, and elsewhere show that those raising their voices want to be heard. It is the responsibility of the campus administration to take them seriously, to be better prepared for the next time, and to keep the board informed. Such events can be "teachable moments" when the president can express concerns and underscore the need for both respect of others and freedom of speech.

Presidential Searches and Hiring

Academic presidents benefit from having a broad and diverse background of experiences. Boards should consider candidates from a variety of professions. The essential considerations are intellectual curiosity, the ability to communicate clearly and coherently in writing and speaking, a desire to listen, respect for higher education values and traditions as well as for others, and a commitment to the institution's mission and integrity.

The search for a new president requires careful planning by the board. The board will organize a search committee that will consist of five to seven trustees, one or two of whom will chair or co-chair the search. The remainder of the committee typically will consist of a senior dean, two faculty, and two students (one undergraduate and one in a graduate program on campus), or some close approximation to this model.

An executive search firm may be of assistance. Both not-for-profit and for-profit firms can be helpful. As with any other consultant, success depends upon the clarity of the assignment; the leadership of the trustee chair or co-chair, the president, and/or provost in the search; and the commitment of the search committee to adhere to the goals and criteria of the search. Be flexible about deadlines. It is more important to find the right person, even if it requires extending the deadline, than it is to make a mistake by being fixed to a date.

While the board probably thinks it wants a president who will serve seven to ten years, there is a particular challenge if the new president will be succeeding someone who has served a long time. The departing president may have become a beloved figure on campus, made agreements that limit the college's flexibility, or presided over several years of declining enrollments and fiscal distress. In these and similar cases, it may be prudent to find an interim president, perhaps someone from the campus who can guide a transition period. More likely, the goal will be to find someone sponsored by an organization such as AGB or the Registry for College and University Presidents in order to find an experienced president who will assume leadership for one to three years. Following this interim period, the board could begin thinking about a longer-serving executive leader.

The board will most likely delegate the task of soliciting and interviewing potential search firms to the trustees on the search committee or to a subset of the executive committee. There are many firms that specialize in searching for higher education leadership positions. The board chair or another designated person might ask the trustees of other institutions for the names of firms used, or ask the campus president or board administrator to compile profiles of several firms to be reviewed. If one of the trustees is from higher education, he or she probably has knowledge of the available firms.

It is essential to interview the firm's representative thoroughly. What is the background of the person assigned to your search? Will he or she be available to you when you need them, or do they have four other searches underway at the same time? What methods do they use to search?

The next task of the committee and the board is to prepare and agree on a briefing document for the search committee and the consultant. This document should include a profile of the institution; the needs and priorities of the campus; a data book of information about the institution, its peers and competitors, and its models for aspirational goals; the suggested profile of experiences, skills, abilities, and values of the successful candidate; any particular expectations for the post; and the compensation and benefits for the position. In other words, the board must define the job to be done in a way that candidates can be screened and the successful candidate can be evaluated. It is not unreasonable for the board to be inquisitive about a candidate's physical and financial health, but background checks are better left to the search firm, which would know the legal parameters of such inquiries.

The goal of the search committee and the search consultant is to search by means of advertisements, letters and telephone calls to potential prospects, communication with national associations, and requests to the campus community and alumni to suggest potential candidates. The search must be active; the screening of applicants and nominees is not the only task.

Setting the salary and benefits for the president, and the process by which the compensation will be reviewed in the future, is important to do at this point. Candidates will want to know, of course, and the board needs to be clear on its policy. There are guidelines for setting both salary and benefits, and they should be followed. The board does not want the state or federal IRS asking questions that might not have defensible answers.

Compensation usually includes not only salary and normal benefits, but also an official residence on or near campus in which the president is required to live and host official functions, or a housing allowance for a residence that can be used in the same way. Some campuses have historic houses and require that the president and his or her family allow tours during certain hours. It is best practice for the board to authorize and complete any renovations to the university-owned house and the president's office before the new president moves in so that he or she will not be branded as extravagant because of the upgrade to the facilities. Many presidents have gotten into trouble on campus and in the community because the board did not tend to such renovations earlier. Deferred compensation is a normal perquisite, but country club memberships can raise eyebrows. Also, membership in other forms of private club can be problematic, especially if the club has restrictive membership policies.

The board and the search committee should have a clear understanding of the role to be played by the president's spouse, whether male or female. Will they be expected to have responsibilities for the campus? Will there be expectations for or limitations on their involvement in the community or their profession? Will they have an office, staff, or compensation? These are questions to be answered before anyone is interviewed.

Once the search is underway, the focus will be on finding the right person by reviewing the paperwork of candidates, selecting a dozen or so for off-campus or so-called airport interviews, and preparing a short list of finalists to visit the campus and meet the senior officers, deans, and faculty and student leaders.

Hiring a campus president is a major commitment. If it takes longer to find someone who seems perfect, take the time. There are consequences for not being thorough. A failed presidential search can be an expensive proposition, especially when the selected candidate is not a good fit for the campus culture and expectations. Therefore, it is wise to take the time necessary to be thorough and thoughtful.

During this period, the board is focused on the search and the future president. When the new president is selected and announced, complications can arise. While there are a few articles about the last six months of the outgoing president's time, there is not much guidance regarding the sensitive relationships among the board, the departing president, and the incoming president following the announcement of the president-elect up to the final day in office of the sitting president. Yet all three parties need guidance and a plan in order to avoid confusion and bad feelings.

The board and the departing president must concentrate on the responsibilities at hand, even as the incoming president is asking for information from the vice presidents and other staff. The campus presidency is a full-time job, so plans have to be made about when and how often the sitting president will be available to brief the incoming president and help prepare for the transition. And the incoming president must be ready with questions. Transitions are two-way transactions.

Avoiding Presidential Turnover

Good governance is critical for the success of the campus president. However, the turnover among college presidents seems to be increasing. Pressures from internal and external stakeholders, including the governor's office, and from tighter budgets due to decreased net tuition revenue, increased demands for fundraising, and student life issues, are resulting in what one author has called "the job nobody can keep."[2]

For example, among historically black colleges and universities, nearly one-third of presidencies, or 34 of 107, ended either through termination or resignation during the 2015-2016 academic year.[3] According to another study, "a majority of college business officers . . . think higher education is an industry under siege" because of changes in political spending and new trends in college-going.[4] Overall, the turnover is of concern not only for the instability it creates, but also because provosts, those in the traditional pipeline for the top job, are less interested in it. According to one report, just 30 percent of provosts are interested in being promoted to president.[5] The turnover also is of concern because the skills these campus leaders need are changing.

At a conference session on the skills and attributes needed for a successful campus presidency, the respondents cited the following as essential: "risk-taker, visionary, passionate about educational access for students, data driven, and strategic communicator."[6] The lack of this last attribute was cited as one reason for the decline in public support for higher education. It also has been said that we lack presidents with a national platform who promote the role of higher education as a public good and of service to society.[7] In an effort to deal with this lack, some institutions have sought presidents from outside academia who were thought to be strategic communicators (including politicians and corporate executives). The results of these searches are mixed. Yet, if those in the traditional pipeline of provosts and deans are not interested in taking on the presidency, as the data suggest, then colleges and universities are going to have to find new sources of candidates for this complicated job.

The search for a new president is not any easy task. I recall a search where two of the four finalists for the position at a modestly sized liberal arts college with a few master's degree programs located in a suburb called to ask me about the campus and the board. During the conversations, I realized that neither one was the right fit and would not take the post even if offered. I concluded this because one, who lived in a city about three hours away where her spouse was partner in a large law firm, asked if she had to be on campus each weekend. I said, it is a "24-7" post with many activities on weekends. The other candidate was provost at a large, doctoral-granting university and was a candidate to be president at a large urban institution. I knew from her past roles that this was the kind of presidency she wanted. I called the board chair, whom I knew, to tell him of my conversations. He said, "That's too bad, as one of the other candidates just withdrew, leaving us with just one." I asked about this remaining candidate and, hearing doubts in the board chair's voice, recommended just continuing the search. "I can't," he said, "we already have interviewed him three times." He was concerned about delaying a decision after all the time and effort in interviewing this candidate and the expectations that these meetings raised with the person and the campus. I advised him that it would be better to extend the search than to make a mistake, but he and his board went forward. The candidate lasted fewer than two years in office. He was not the right person for the campus and that quickly became evident.

In another case, the chair of the board became co-chair of the presidential search committee and promised to complete the search by November 1. When an unexpected choice for president was announced, a member of the search committee talked confidentially about the process and the final four candidates. The committee selected the person, it was said, who was the "best prepared for the interview." This is not the same as being best prepared for the job, but a deadline had been set and finishing on time became the goal.

In addition, I know of a board member who recounted his regret about a search in which he did not ask the successful candidate about his aspirations for the future. When this president left after ten months to take the top post in a university system where for many years he had been a faculty member and campus president, everyone was shocked by his departure but not surprised by his choice. The trustee regretted not asking the candidate why he was interested in what was, in fact, a very different institution from the one he had left and which was the one he returned to lead.

I know of searches for presidents and other campus leadership positions that took extra time because the person who seemed to be the best candidate wanted a much higher salary than officials thought the position deserved compared to other positions on campus and at neighboring institutions. In other cases, the people who seemed the best prepared simply could not afford the cost of living in the area. In each case, the search was delayed and took longer, much to the chagrin of some trustees. Again, it pays to invest in the search and be confident in the person found rather than be invested in meeting what is, after all, usually an arbitrary deadline.

If the traditional route through the provost's office is not as great a source for future campus leaders as it once was, where will presidents be found? What more can be done to create on-campus leadership development programs for future university officers? How can the search process be improved to ensure greater success in finding talented and successful leaders? How might succession planning on campus be improved so that both boards and presidents can weather sudden changes in leadership? The board should consider these questions during the search for a president.

Managing Presidential Transitions

Boards should understand that the relationship between the outgoing and incoming president can be fraught with anxieties and other emotions. Perhaps that is why someone composed this fable to describe the relations between the two:

> An outgoing president prepared three envelopes with different messages for the incoming president and left them in the office desk with instructions not to open them until there was a problem. Early in the new president's tenure, there was a crisis, so he or she opened the first envelope. The message said simply, "Blame your predecessor." Later in the year, or perhaps the next year, there was another crisis, and the president under fire opened the second envelope. This time the message read, "Reorganize." The president announced a reorganization plan, and the campus quieted down. After all, the president demonstrated who was in charge. When a third crisis occurred, as they sometimes do, the president opened the remaining envelope and was surprised to read this simple message: "Prepare three envelopes."

Following a successful search for a new president, the board chair or designee should help guide the transition. The incoming person will want to learn as much as possible about the university and prepare for his or her first months in office. In this period, the new president must be careful not to interfere with current plans or give mixed signals to continuing staff members. The board chair must be alert to this possibility. It is not up to the departing president to assume full responsibility for the transition.

A model used in some cases is for a long-serving and successful president to assume the title of chancellor and assist the new president and board in fundraising and alumni relations. This is a way to maintain good relations with alumni and have ready access to someone with deep knowledge of the institution. Another method of guidance may come in the form of a memorandum from the outgoing president (see Appendix G for a template transition memorandum). This memorandum should discuss the following items, at least:

- Personnel matters that are pending, such as the removal of a dean or senior officer if the incumbent were to continue, thus freeing the new president from such action early in the first year
- Policy concerns that were being discussed but not resolved, such as a change in admissions or financial aid policies, or when the facilities master plan should be updated
- Donor prospects who were being nurtured so that there is no lapse in communication and stewardship with actual or potential donors, including how the new president would like the emeritus president to help, if at all
- Any planned reviews of an outside consultant's work

In addition, each campus has delicate relations with the local community. The departing president, who no doubt has developed relations with these people over the years, may want to ensure that the incoming president is introduced to neighbors, elected officials, and the head of the regional chamber of commerce as soon as practical, even during one of the preparatory visits to campus before the official arrival date.

These items, as well as observations about the operations of the board, are important to discuss openly and fully in order to ensure a smooth transition. Again, it takes a receptive incoming president and a board that accepts its responsibilities for the transition to make this work.

It is also essential that the president and the board have a clear understanding of the provisions in the president's employment agreement. There have been unfortunate incidents in which language that had been agreed upon, even for years, was given new interpretation by the board chair at the time of transition. Such provisions include when the outgoing president must vacate the president's house, what staff and financial support will be available during a sabbatical year if there is one, and what titles, privileges, and responsibilities the departing president will have. Will there be an official portrait of the departing president? He or she should not have to ask. There is a diversity of practices experienced by outgoing presidents.

While the range in treatment of outgoing presidents is varied, the range of activities of those leaving is equally wide. In addition to those who return to the faculty to teach, some become executive search or coaching consultants, others become foundation executives, still others become permanent or interim presidents elsewhere, many write books, and some truly retire. When a president leaves, there can be a vacuum in leadership, even with a new president soon to arrive. It is important for the board to discuss this with the incoming president and perhaps the provost, as it is not unusual to see flatterers emerge who will attempt to curry favor from whoever is in charge. Sometimes the overtures are sincere, but sometimes not. Machiavelli was correct in advising that flatterers should be shunned.[8]

Some presidents have experienced boards who thought that offers of assistance to the incoming president were signs of wanting to "hang on," an unwillingness or inability to let go. It should be understood that the outgoing president has probably devoted twenty-four hours a day, seven days a week, for many years, in service to the institution and wants to be helpful—and treated fairly. This does not mean he or she wants to cling to the office or be in the way. In fact, the outgoing president should be considered as a fount of institutional memory and personal, not just institutional, relationships with alumni and friends. To tell the outgoing president that he or she no longer represents the university may be accurate as an official statement, but any lack of responsiveness by him or her toward alumni and other donors could reflect poorly on the institution.

So, while the outgoing chief executive of a company may be treated as "yesterday's news," the outgoing president of a college, unless he or she was forced out, should be treated as an asset, a bearer of the institution's heritage. This may be difficult for trustees with backgrounds in business and finance to comprehend. Boards should remember that the university is a moral institution, one with values and a respect for history, more similar to a multigeneration, family-owned business than to a modern stock-traded corporation.

The range of respect given to outgoing presidents varies widely. For example, a president who retired after twenty-eight years at the helm of a relatively large private university and planned to write a history of the institution was told by his successor that he could not have access to the university's archives to do his research. Another was told that the title president emeritus had no meaning and he should not be seen as representing the institution, even though alumni still invited him to dine with them. Another who had been highly successful over twenty-two years and retired to the faculty was never consulted by the new president—even though the former president had raised large sums of money and was beloved by major donors as well as other alumni. At the other end of the spectrum, Cornell University had three retired presidents on its faculty at one time in recent years. When a new president died unexpectedly in her first year, there was an already-prepared "interim" president teaching on campus.

Succession Planning for the Executive Team

The campus president should prepare and update an executive team succession plan memorandum for discussion with the board and for commentary during his or her annual review. The memorandum should specify the kinds of leadership development needed and planned for the vice presidents (and even deans), how to fill in for or replace senior staff members who leave or are incapacitated for a period of time, and ways to enhance the diversity of the team (see Appendix H for a model succession planning memorandum).

Sometimes, board members will want the president to hire "seconds" to vice presidents who are of nearly equal talent and caliber. This is expensive. Most organizations cannot afford redundancy in senior positions. The best approach is to have a second who can fulfill the responsibilities of the post until a full-time replacement is found. If he or she can actually do the job effectively following this period as the interim, so much the better. Rather than taking a prescriptive approach by telling the president what should be done, board members should ask the president about the plans for succession.

Chapter 5

Strategic Leadership

There is no cookie-cutter approach to governance, even though the basic principles apply universally to institutions of all types, two year and four year, undergraduate and graduate, public and private. While some people refer to strategic plans, others refer to long-range plans, and still others to five-year and even twenty-year plans. The important point is for the institution to have a plan that is readable and credible, including guidance for setting priorities and measuring progress. The important task is to engage in strategic or reflective thinking before formulating a plan.

Dick Chait and his colleagues at Harvard have outlined three types of boards and the manner in which they help guide their institutions.[1] The first type is the board dedicated to *compliance* or *control* as its first priority. He compares this type of board, metaphorically, to a dam on a river or to a landlord toward a tenant. These boards cover four of the five basic roles of good governance: setting policy, hiring the CEO, raising money, and acting as the fiduciary fiscal agent.

The second type covers these duties and adds another dimension. The *strategic* or direction-setter board sets the mission, vision, and direction of the organization, acting as a steering device, like a rudder for a boat or a compass for a navigator.

The third type of board is *generative*, meaning that it acts as the vision setter while guiding implementation; it charts the values that guide choices. This board focuses on meaningful work, creates legitimacy, provides stature, and encourages vigilance as well as collaborative thinking. It provides funding, but also intellectual, reputational, political, and social capital. It influences the culture to be one of aspiration and transparency. This type of board engages in strategic thinking (i.e., it assesses assumptions, not just goals and strategies). These trustees are reflective practitioners who think about what they are doing and why they are doing it. Darryl Greer describes this board type as *prospective*; its style is "anticipatory" and is "explicit, open, and accountable."[2] This type of board is a partner to the president.

Ten Habits of Highly Effective Boards

Richard Legon of the Association of Governing Boards of Universities and Colleges (AGB) detailed the following ten habits of highly effective boards in response to questions about university trustee effectiveness as posed by policy leaders, business executives, accreditors, and others:

- Create a culture of inclusion
- Uphold basic fiduciary principles
- Cultivate a healthy relationship with the president
- Select an effective board chair
- Establish an effective governance committee
- Delegate appropriate decision-making authority to committees
- Consider strategic risk factors
- Provide appropriate oversight of academic quality
- Develop a renewed commitment to shared governance
- Focus on accountability[3]

It is the responsibility of the board to approve and monitor strategic plans. A basic question to be discussed in orientation sessions and board meetings is *What is the model for a better version of our institution?* As follow-up questions: What will it take to achieve this model? What are the implications for the students and faculty recruited and supported, the programs and services provided, the resources needed, and the reward and cost structure of the institution?

Strategic plans are about principles for decision-making, priorities for action, and milestones for monitoring progress. The board should know the principles, ideally developed by consensus, by which decisions will be made. Are the principles rooted in a culture of shared governance, or does the board make all decisions with little delegation? Any plan should start with institutional purpose (i.e., the mission of the institution) and with an understanding of the heritage, culture, and values upon which the future is being built.

Next, the plan should identify the principles for decision-making and the priorities for action; assumptions about internal and external forces at work (a SWOT analysis of strengths, weaknesses, opportunities, and threats); alternative courses of action; results desired and resources needed; strategies for achieving goals; and milestones and metrics for monitoring progress, knowing that some goals are subjective and cannot be measured with numbers. An environmental scan should analyze why students do and do not accept offers of admission, the institution's price competitiveness, and the comparative advantages of the institution.

The plan should also include periods of time for reflection and a community-wide review of goals and progress. Communication during the process is essential. Every plan should identify who is responsible for different parts of the strategies and the timetable for achieving the stated goals. In the end, though, the president is the chief planning officer.

The board should know the points of leverage available to it and to campus leaders to make progress. Each point of leverage represents an opportunity to use normal activities to support the achievement of goals:

- Mission statement
- Trustee agenda
- Strategic plan
- Annual academic program and administrative unit reviews
- Annual goals and objectives for senior officers, including deans
- Annual budget requests and allocations
- Staffing plans and decisions
- Funds for faculty and curriculum development
- Annual awards, rewards, and other forms of recognition for meritorious service, including honorary degrees
- Five- and ten-year regional accrediting self-studies
- Fundraising case statements of priorities

Survey results by BoardMax[4] suggest that a satisfying board experience is related to the effectiveness of the board. The simplest and yet most fundamental characteristic is showing up (i.e., attendance at board and committee meetings and celebratory occasions). Such attendance is related to board satisfaction and a feeling of effectiveness. This is to be expected. If members are not satisfied, they probably will not show up. If they do not show up, they will not learn the reasons to celebrate.

Celebratory events can bring joy to board members as well as to the students and faculty who are central to them. These include Matriculation Day (or an equivalent event to open the fall semester) and Graduation Day. Such ceremonies underscore the notion of togetherness and a commitment to a mission with a history. The faculty processional, the wearing of robes with hoods of different colors to signify different institutions and subjects of study, the carrying of the mace and other regalia related to the history of the institution, and the singing of the alma mater all signify that those gathered are part of an academic community and a higher education culture that spans centuries. This reminder of an institution's history and its place in the higher education firmament emphasizes to each generation of students that it is part of something bigger than the present and that the students, and the faculty, staff, and trustees, are part of a legacy that they will help carry on.

Board members want to know that their ideas are heard and welcomed, just as faculty and students do. At each meeting, and on an annual questionnaire, members' views about board operations should be solicited. It is important for the president to be in touch with each board member on a routine basis, whether in person, by phone, or at least by email. We ask a great deal of board members, including their commitment of time, intellect, experiences, and resources in support of the institution, and we should show them the respect and support they deserve. Board members will not be satisfied if the board chair is a powerful person who takes control without listening to others or is someone whom members abide simply because he or she is a singularly notable person in society or a major donor to the university.

Trustees can also be engaged on campus to give talks about their careers and to meet informally with students, faculty, and staff. A board is composed of members with certain talents and experiences to support the university, and there should be more chances to meet the people—students, faculty and staff—who give life to the campus. Benefiting from the board's talents in the boardroom is not enough.

Board members want to feel that they have truly influenced the direction of the campus. By helping to make strategic influences on student life (such as in the case of fraternities, investment policies, or facilities development), board members can become more engaged and enthusiastic for the remainder of their terms. Board members who are engaged and satisfied are more likely to invest in the university and recruit new prospects for consideration as members and donors.

Board Retreats

Once every year or so, the board should meet in a retreat format, which may require an additional time commitment from members. For example, if the board normally meets for one day, the retreat format may add another day and evening. With more time together, the board can engage in deeper discussions about broad issues, learn more about the life of students and faculty on campus, and get to know each other better without having the pressure of making decisions within a short time frame. The regular business of faculty appointments, reappointments, tenure, promotion, and leaves of absence; operating and capital budgets; and related items need action and take time. The board also needs time for deliberation, which the retreat format allows.

These deeper discussions should take on the character of a seminar, with strategic visioning about the institution and its governance, and about the role and expectations of the trustees. A central part of the discussion should be a focus on what is needed for the institution to continue to improve, with attention to the institution's goals, the reason for these goals, and the requirements for success in achieving them.

It is often helpful to include an outside speaker for part of the retreat. Potential topics might include an overview of demographic trends in the region, such as ethnicity, economics, and behaviors in college enrollment; changes in employment opportunities in the region(s) served by the institution; trends in using technological aids to enhance student learning; new laws and regulations affecting good governance practices; opportunities for cost sharing with other institutions; and so on. The board could also engage a campus scholar who knows the campus's history and invite him or her to describe periods of significant change in the past. The board can then discuss the relevance of the historical events to contemporary challenges. These and other topics can form the basis of a stimulating discussion, especially to inform strategic planning.

Metrics

One way for a board to keep track of progress is to establish a dashboard with goals, metrics, benchmarks, and a timeline for monitoring progress. Nevertheless, it is important for the board to know and acknowledge that not everything of value can be measured. Some subjective, professional judgments are required.

I recall a meeting at which I was presenting the latest version of a dashboard, which had been advocated over several meetings by a particular board member. The chart had twenty-three items on it, with metrics for each showing the goal, the benchmark, and the current status. I tried to explain to the board how this tool worked to keep track of the activities of a complex organization. It was not an easy task. At the meeting, a board member who was the retired chairman and CEO of a major corporation interrupted me and asked, "Which of these twenty-three items keeps you up at night? Shouldn't we focus on those and see how the board can help?"

This response was perfect. This is just how a board should participate as a partner, through questions rather than prescriptions. This also helped avoid a common plague of "paralysis by analysis" through over-use of evaluation tools.

Consultants

University presidents cannot and should not act alone. In addition to the board as partner in governance, the president's advisory council as independent advisors, and the senior staff of vice presidents and deans as a president's cabinet, it is often helpful to engage paid consultants to assist in strategic planning and other activities. There are many types of consultants. Some are affiliated with AGB, some with national academic discipline associations, others are from private fundraising firms, and still others are independent contractors.

When I arrived at Adelphi as the sixth president in three and one-half years, I learned that there had been two previous strategic planning exercises that surveyed the entire campus and resulted in two large volumes. Unfortunately, neither included a concise list of key findings and recommendations. Instead, there were numerous recommendations with no structured way for either the board of trustees or faculty leadership to monitor progress on priorities.

I knew we needed a strategic plan, but I also knew that the campus was tired of "strategic planning." Therefore, I engaged a firm to assist me in listening to campus constituents comment on strengths, weaknesses, opportunities, and threats, as well as priorities for action. The members of the firm interviewed faculty, staff, and students, and learned about policies that seemed sensible at first blush, including a mandate against playing sports on the well-manicured lawns, but that in fact interfered with student play such as Frisbee throwing and resulted in student dissatisfaction. We were able to undo such policies, allow students to enjoy the campus, maintain beautiful green spaces, and improve the retention rate.

There also were concerns about the quality of academic programs resulting from previous personnel policies and budget decisions. We brought in experts from academe and industry to review curricula and staffing, and to suggest opportunities for strengthening programs and student experiences. The reports guided the development of certain programs, the cancellation of others, and the identification of strengths on which to create new programs and partnerships.

We also engaged consultants on board governance and operations. At one session, when the topic of micromanagement was to be discussed, the two worst offenders said, almost in unison, "We can pass on this; it is not a problem here." The consultant did not skip over the topic, and everyone benefitted from a robust discussion.

Consultants can also provide helpful guidance when building alumni relations programs or developing fundraising capacity, such as the design of annual giving programs or a comprehensive capital campaign. One consultant whom we engaged helped us develop a statement of expectations for the board and was a terrific coach for the staff and a helpful advisor to me as president. I must say, however, that the board was often uneasy when she advised them on the role they should play in fundraising. She could and did challenge them about fundraising in ways that I as president found problematic given my relationship with the board. We were very successful in fundraising, and I give her a lot of credit.

I also engaged a consultant to serve as a coach for me when I became concerned about certain forces on the board. The coach, an expert on governance, was helpful, and I helped him expand his business portfolio. I saw him every other month or so, and he became a confidential sounding board. I could try out ideas with him before talking with the senior staff, my advisory council, or the trustees.

Once, when a vice president was exhibiting difficult behavior toward other vice presidents, I offered to hire a coach. The person agreed, and we discussed two possible choices. We chose one, and off we went. When I told the board what I was doing, one member asked me why I thought the behavior would change. I said that I was not sure it would, but I felt an obligation to try. The behavior did not change, but not because of the coach. I had to part ways with someone I had hired.

The benefits of consultants are numerous. The campus audit firm should be an obvious source of consulting assistance. In addition to conducting the annual audit and advising on internal audit functions such as administrative operations reviews, they can advise on enterprise risk measures, fraud prevention, and comparative data for benchmarking.

Consultants provide another set of eyes and ears to see and hear what may be held back from the president and the board either intentionally or unintentionally. They also allow the president to extend his or her reach by providing additional help in communicating with and listening to various campus constituents.

Consultants can guide campus leadership in a number of fields, including government relations, public relations, advertising and marketing, architecture, space planning, and construction management. Faculty and alumni with expertise in the field should be asked to serve on the planning committee. They will know what questions to ask and will likely be critical of the results if they have not been consulted before the plans are adopted and executed. If an institution is seeking accreditation, the accrediting association may provide a consultant to assist in the development of a self-study and initiatives for improvement.

Developing Leadership

As Warren Bennis said, "One of the most reliable indicators and predictors of true leadership is an individual's ability to find meaning in negative events and to learn from even the most trying circumstances."[5] When it comes to leadership, emotional intelligence is an essential ingredient. The elements of emotional intelligence include *self-awareness*, which means listening to signs of our physical and mental health even as we listen to others; *self-regulation*, which means being able to disagree without being disagreeable; *motivation*, which means being inspired and inspiring others; and *empathy*, which means being aware of and open to others who may be different from us.

Leadership is a system consisting of three components: the leader, the followers, and the context. Barbara Kellerman says the *leader* must be effective, ethical, important to the cause, and consequential in decisions and actions.[6] The *followers* are not lemmings, but might be categorized as participants, activists, bystanders, and diehards. The *context* might be historical, cultural, psychological, or institutional.

In order for a board to help the president develop appropriate leadership skills and abilities, it must know the characteristics of an ethical, effective campus leader, starting with character. Good leaders for a campus or any other organization must be committed to transparency, integrity, and fairness. They must have an ability to listen and the willingness to learn. Principled leaders have a moral or ethical relationship with others based on trust, mutual interests, and obligations to an institution greater than any one person.

It is the leaders' responsibility to create and encourage a culture of conscience, not just a commitment to compliance. Effective leaders do not just espouse a theory of ethics, but demonstrate good ethical practices. This is true for the board as well. Good governance demands transparency and integrity in decision-making. Boards should be mindful about campus leaders who become lauded as icons. We have seen this happen with college coaches like Bobby Knight and Joe Paterno, and with executives like Jack Welch. No one should be above the law or above the campus or corporate code of conduct. Yet too often we seem to ascribe legendary dimension to successful coaches and executives who then think they are above the standards that others must follow.

The board should also see to it that the president has opportunities for professional development. It is important for campus presidents to have a wide variety of experiences. In addition to programs for new presidents at places like Harvard and programs for continuing presidents such as meetings of the American Council on Education, the Association of Governing Boards, and the associations for private and public colleges, there are worthwhile programs at the American Management Association. Such programs provide opportunities to learn more about leadership while participating in sessions where teamwork and role play are important adjuncts to reading, lectures, and seminars.

Good sources of professional development for presidents and provosts are national associations, such as the American Council on Education (ACE), the Association of Governing Boards (AGB), the National Association of Independent Colleges and Universities (NAICU), the American Association of State Colleges and Universities (AASCU), the Council of Independent Colleges (CIC), the Association of Public and Land-Grant Universities (APLU), and the American Association of Community Colleges (AACC). The American Association of Colleges and Universities (AACU) is a terrific source of ideas about teaching and learning for both senior academic officers and faculty leaders.

A board should be as intentional about leadership development for its members as it is for the president. Just as the president is responsible for the professional development of his or her direct reports, and they in turn are responsible for the development of their direct reports, the board chair and chair of the trustee affairs committee should guide the board and the president in their professional development. There should be opportunities for each to participate in programs at national higher education association meetings, read higher education journals and newsletters, and learn from consultants brought to campus for board and leadership development.

The identification of opportunities for leadership growth and advancement in knowledge about good governance practices is a major part of the board's duties. Fulfilling this duty can assure the availability of the kinds of talent needed for the continued strengthening of the board and leadership team. The trustee affairs committee should consider board succession planning as it contemplates the membership and leadership of board committees. Rotating members and preparing them for committee leadership, as well as speaking on behalf of the board at ceremonial occasions, can help prepare future board leadership.

The literature on leadership development is voluminous. Various authors have written about "essential attributes" and "universal styles." Many such books are listed in the bibliography. This guide establishes four elements of leadership: listening, reading, speaking, and writing.

Listening can mean seeking both formal and informal times to hear people comment on how things are going and what they wish could be improved. Presidents listen by walking the halls and pathways, attending events, and otherwise putting themselves in a position to hear from students, faculty, staff, alumni, employers, vendors, and others. When listening, leaders pay attention and learn; they do not just wait their turn to rebut what was said. Listening carefully also includes watching intently to pay attention to physical expressions, to acknowledge one's partner, and to affirm what has been heard. Active listening requires memory as well as comprehension. Machiavelli was correct when he said, "Be a great asker, and a patient hearer of the truth."[7]

Another way to take in information, ideas, and inspiration is by *reading*. Not all reading is equal. Presidents need to keep up with the news and informed opinion, they need to know about the latest technologies and developments in science, and they need to know what is happening in higher education policy and practice. Presidents should also read history in order to understand context, biographies to learn how others have faced challenges, and fiction and poetry to see imaginations soar and find new ways of refining their use of language and imagery. History, biography, and fiction, followed by reflection, are good sources for presidents to find meaning in their own lives.

Presidents also express themselves through *speech*. Every campus president gives speeches, talks, and welcoming comments to groups of all types and sizes. These are opportunities for college leaders to express values, emphasize the unique features of the institution, and tell stories that illustrate how the mission is being fulfilled. These stories become like fables, legends that illuminate the history and heritage of the campus. Every talk, whether spontaneous or prepared, whether short or long, should have a message beyond "Welcome." Each is an opportunity to broadcast the mission, vision, and unique nature of the institution. Such speeches are usually more effective when they are authored and delivered with personal passion rather than scripted by a professional speechwriter. Sometimes, speaking is in the form of a request for help. Leaders should not be afraid to do so. At other times, speaking is part of a negotiation on some issue. Such speaking may become compromise, but a compromise of position does not necessarily mean a compromise of principles. Indeed, compromises are necessary for democratic processes to work, even on a college campus.

Finally, *writing* is an essential art for effective leadership. Since most college presidents come up through the ranks of academia, they have written scholarly articles and books, but mostly for relatively narrow audiences that often have a vocabulary of their own. Campus leaders should be encouraged to write for publication in more popular outlets as well as in professional journals. Writing op-ed pieces for the daily or weekly newspaper or an e-newsletter is good practice. It is a form of teaching, with the general public instead of a group of professional colleagues or students as the audience. Such writing can raise the profile of the institution as well as of the individual.

Alumni, of course, constitute another audience. The president should share with them his or her thoughts on important issues related to higher education and society, especially as they relate to the campus. Maintaining an email list, a blog, or a Twitter account for colleagues, alumni, and friends on and off campus is an effective way to communicate with many people simultaneously. Through this widespread communication, campus leaders can inform, influence, and encourage others; promote worthy ideas; and engage a wide range of readers in an ongoing discussion that connects them to the campus.

Of course not all writing is of an intellectual bent. The president should send handwritten notes of congratulations and condolence to campus faculty, staff, students, and alumni, and often to parents of students. These expressions of congratulations, thanks, or grief will be appreciated and reflect well on the person, the office, and the campus. There are no small gestures.

The president and his or her staff will also write or call those who have written or called in anger about some policy or practice. The best advice is to acknowledge the complaint quickly, even by telephone, and to contact the person again when information is available for a more complete response. All too often the inclination is to reply after the investigation, which can take days or weeks, by which time a complaint about the lack of response takes center stage. I recall an instance when we received a complaint about course registration for adult students from a person in a nearby town. It turned out that she had previously served in the registrar's office at an institution in another state. I called to say I would check into her complaint and later learned that her suggestion improved our procedures and resulted in increased enrollment of returning and adult students.

Developing effective board and executive leadership is an ongoing responsibility and should be taken seriously. It should be an important part of the annual performance reviews of the board chair, the board as a whole, and the president.

Chapter 6

Leading Higher Education into the Future

Forces for Change

If we look again at the variables of population, politics, and public policy that seem to have shaped university growth in the United States, what might these variables suggest about forces for change in the future?

We certainly face issues of population, although today the issue is no longer about the movement of populations to frontier territories. Today, there are potential students of all ages who live in rural areas and in urban centers and who lack access to postsecondary opportunities. Another change in population dynamics is represented by the increase in nontraditional students, who are now the majority in higher education. The eighteen- to twenty-four-year-old cohort is the minority. Forty percent of students attend community colleges; only 14 percent live on campus. The majority of students who have been out of school for years have jobs and families, are more likely to enroll part-time, and often have difficulty in managing class schedules. They also are more demographically diverse, often coming from under-served communities and the first in their families to attempt college. Trustees should be aware of how their institutions are organized to serve these nontraditional students with nontraditional policies and practices.[1]

Another force with which to contend is the rising "populism" in public policy debates and the consequent change in priorities for public funding, even when studies indicate the need to increase the percentage of the population with a college education. With prisons and pensions squeezing the funding for higher education, colleges and universities must find more effective ways to advocate for the societal as well as the individual benefits of higher education and ways to change their cost structures, including more collaborative arrangements for sharing expenses. An effort at restructuring costs must be taken in order to reduce tuition discounting as a way of providing financial assistance and merit scholarship aid. In addition, campuses must find new sources of revenue beyond that which students can bring without diminishing institutional commitments to purpose and mission.

Other shifts shaping the future of higher education in the United States include the number of high school graduates; the income and employment status of students and families; whether students will study full-time or part-time; whether students will be in residence on campus, live off campus, or attend online; and students' career focus. Forecasters have proposed varying models of institutional development for the future. Some campuses will scale back in size of enrollment or decide to grow through mergers; others will become more specialized and focused; still others will change to be fully online; and some will attempt to become a hybrid combination of all types.

Other forces for change include federal and state policies, including initiatives for "free" tuition at public colleges, the lack of clarity for the value proposition of higher education in view of its costs, and challenges to the campus climate due to heightened political tensions. There also are more global forces, including students and faculty moving among countries, institutions building campuses and partnerships with universities in other countries, and information and data moving freely around the world.

Finally, major forces for change are found in the technological breakthroughs that can support teaching and learning and gain efficiencies in back-office processing functions. One of the top drivers of costs in higher education, after tuition discounting, compensation, and health care costs, is the investment made in technology. There are always new technologies, and some institutions attempt to keep up with the latest equipment without an adequate plan for its use. While it is important to have up-to-date technology so that students are prepared for its use while in college and after graduation, it also is important to have a strategy for how technology investments will enhance student learning and faculty teaching. There is a maxim that bears attention: *Be on the leading edge, not the bleeding edge.* Some campuses spend money on technology in ineffective ways. The college's audit firm can help the board evaluate the campus technology plan, including how the institution might anticipate the benefits of new technologies for improvements in course content, pedagogy, and student learning.

Technological advances will prompt further changes in policies for student course credit transfer and new forms of credentialing, among other policies. Online learning can be used for distance education or to support blended courses that combine online with in-class instruction, as well as for "flipped" classes in which students use online and other resources prior to class time. This allows class time to be used for discussion and group projects. Communications technologies can facilitate student and faculty interactions.

The same technologies that can be used to facilitate teaching and learning and to improve administrative efficiencies are being used by new providers of credentials to challenge the traditional ways of organizing college curricula and providing instruction. Lessons can and must be learned from them in both how to achieve goals and what pitfalls to avoid, especially with regard to aggressive recruiting and revenue diversity.

These various forces challenge us to think anew about what a university is. A university or college receives a public charter and is more than information alone, like a library or museum; it is more than belief alone, like a church; and it is more than emotion alone, like a club. It is all of these and more. The university is dedicated to the search for evidence-based truths and to the preparation of students as professionals and citizens. The goals of higher education have been to widen access, especially at the undergraduate level, for students of all ages and backgrounds, whether enrolled full-time or part-time, and to promote excellence in teaching and research for the common good.

Goals for a College-Educated Citizenry

The Lumina Foundation, the Gates Foundation, and others have built on this historic foundation and expressed goals for increased college attainment, which they usually link to international comparisons and economic competitiveness, often without mentioning education as a path for more enlightened citizenship. A report by the Lumina Foundation concludes that if current rates of degree and certificate production continue, about 24.2 million Americans, or 40 percent of the population, will earn postsecondary credentials by the year 2025. To reach the foundation's goal of 60 percent, some 16.4 million additional residents will need to be added to that total.[2]

Lumina and others are correct to advocate for more advanced education for more people because the correlation between college attainment, employment status, individual and family stability, citizen engagement, and national economic growth are strong. To reach the goal of 60 percent of citizens having a postsecondary education, however, the United States will need to increase the number of people with at least some college by 50 percent. The only way to do this is to include adult student enrollment in campus planning to a much greater degree than is done now. It will not be possible to achieve this goal with high school students alone. The United States also will need major policy changes in its approach to immigration and immigrants.

In order for opportunities for education and advancement to be further expanded to populations of low-income, minority, and immigrant young people and adults, many of whom live in inner cities, but others of whom live in pockets of rural poverty, there is much that needs to be done through public policy and by universities. Underserved members of our society may experience inadequate schooling because of the lack of public investment in education, housing, nutritious food, and healthcare. These conditions are the result of policies that more often than not benefit the wealthy and exacerbate the condition of the poor. Yet their progress is a public responsibility. Politics and public policies will no doubt encourage new forms of credentialing, especially for job skills, and foster more competition among colleges for students.

In order for the United States to increase the rate of postsecondary education attainment, five principal actors must work in concert.

- First, our society must ensure that all young people enter school ready to learn, following a good night's sleep after studying in a quiet place and having a proper breakfast.
- Second, the nation's schools, from kindergarten through high school, must ensure that all students learn to study and acquire the knowledge, skills, abilities, and values necessary to be active citizens as well as college and career ready.
- Third, state governments must adequately fund public K-12 schools and public colleges and universities as well as need-based financial aid programs so that access and af-

fordability represent promises that can be fulfilled, not just slogans for a campaign. As is shown by the demographic and economic profiles of those attending state universities, subsidized tuition without regard to family income favors the affluent and does little to advance opportunities for those from low-income families.

- Fourth, the federal government must fund the need-based Pell Grant program so that it covers the basic costs of a public university and make income-based loan repayment programs universal.
- Fifth, colleges and universities should be more rigorous in examining the campus cost structure in order to gain efficiencies and improved effectiveness, especially in improving graduation rates, managing deferred maintenance, and growing by substitution rather than by the addition of new programs. They also should ensure that institutional financial aid, even that which is provided through tuition discounting, is focused on the financially neediest students. Colleges should also do more to work with secondary schools in order to facilitate accelerated learning and shorten the time to degree, thus helping families and students save on borrowing. Working locally with schools and communities is just as important as thinking globally as world citizens.

With these steps, we can make greater strides in increasing access to postsecondary opportunities and in improving levels of attainment.

Obstacles to Achieving the Goals

If the primary goal in admitting students is to nurture them to graduation, then the record on graduation rates is a real obstacle to achieving that goal. College dropouts and college debt are connected. The news headlines about college student debt are alarming and suggest that it is out of control. Such articles report on the $1.3 trillion in total college student debt, compare it to consumer debt, and include brief profiles of college seniors and recent graduates carrying debts of $100,000 and more. In fall 2015, some 58 percent of four-year colleges and universities reported that they failed to meet their enrollment targets, and many admissions officers cited concerns about student debt as a major cause of the decline in enrollment.[3]

Before debt is discussed, the federal student loan system must be understood. Federal student loans were started under the National Defense Education Act in 1958, and the program became the Guaranteed Student Loan Program in 1965. The latest version, Direct Lending, was introduced in 1992 and expanded in 1993. In 2007, following reductions in the use of Direct Lending and cutbacks to the federal program in order to increase funding for the Pell Grant program, banks and other nonbank lenders began offering variable-rate student loans with risk pricing of up to 16 percent and more.

It was a combination of these private loans, the fact that student debt may not be cancelled through bankruptcy, the dramatic increase in unprepared students attending private for-profit colleges by using federal and private loans, the desire for graduate study at the master's degree level in order to gain better employment options, and the fact that the federal government did not reduce its interest rates on guaranteed loans, leaving them up to 50 percent higher than many mortgage rates, that caused the surge in total student debt.

In 2012, the average debt load for a recent graduate of a public college was $25,550, 25 percent higher than in 2008. For a private nonprofit college the average debt load was $32,300, 15 percent higher than in 2008. At private for-profit colleges it was $39,950, 26 percent higher than in 2008. The average for all 44-plus million Americans with student-incurred debt is about $37,000.[4]

Media headlines about six-figure student debt do not tell the complete story. This is voluntary debt. There is no reason for anyone to graduate from an undergraduate program with $100,000 or more in debt. Those who do, do so voluntarily, usually in order to pay the tuition and associated costs necessary to attend what they consider to be a prestigious college rather than one that is more affordable. Public college tuition is often 20 percent or more lower than private college tuition, and nearly 50 percent of students in four-year colleges started at two-year community colleges. In fact, only 0.2 percent of student borrowers have $100,000 or more in debt. Of these, 90 percent are in or already have graduated from a graduate school or an advanced professional school like law and medicine. Some 40 percent of all student debt is associated with these students.[5]

This overview should not diminish the negative effects of student debt on college attendance, degree completion, employment choices, and purchasing decisions, such as for housing and appliances. One consequence of dropping out of college is the likelihood of defaulting on student loans. In a recent year, the average student loan default rate for public colleges and universities was 13 percent, and for private non-profit colleges and universities, it was 8.2 percent.[6] At private for-profit colleges, it was 21.8 percent. This is especially problematic for students from low-income families and for those who do not graduate from college, as they likely will earn less and have more trouble repaying their student loans.

Note that students at private for-profit colleges have more debt, higher loan default rates, and lower graduation rates. These are institutions that advocates claim are free-enterprise, market-based alternatives to publicly supported colleges—even as they take more than 90 percent of their revenue from taxpayer sources.[7] While the headlines about student debt do not reveal the true complexity of college student loans, they do suggest some next steps. Colleges should be held accountable for graduation rates, as those who borrow to pay for tuition and do not graduate start at a severe disadvantage compared to others.

The principal drivers of college costs for students and their families are faculty and staff time, financial aid based on merit instead of need, institutional debt for facilities, and cutbacks in state funding. In order to increase the affordability of higher education for middle-income families, there are six steps that can be taken:

1. As an incentive for institutions to do more to control tuition and fee expenses, states could increase the amount of state-based financial aid for institutions that keep net tuition at a certain level relative to average family income. This could provide an added incentive for institutions to be cost sensitive without losing a competitive advantage.
2. Another change that could benefit families is to change the methodology for calculating family assets when determining financial need. Those who save for college should not be disadvantaged compared to those who do not.
3. Colleges and universities can gain efficiencies and cost savings by making more efficient use of facilities. Monday-Wednesday-Friday and Tuesday-Thursday class schedules can leave rooms orphaned unless the class schedule grid is designed for more efficient use.
4. Colleges and universities might pay more attention to student success and retention if they had to repay state and federal financial aid dollars received by students who drop out before graduation. This would encourage institutions to focus on "student fit" as well as on costs, thus becoming more affordable and increasing graduation rates. As this proposal could have a negative effect on the enrollment of low-income students from under-resourced schools, care would need to be taken in preserving the funding of special opportunity programs. We need to ensure that these efforts are sufficiently strong to meet their objectives for access, affordability, and accountability for student success.

5. University reward systems should be mission oriented and student centered. The reward system should give priority to faculty teaching and student learning, even if this means redefining faculty roles. In a university focused on student learning, there should be no conflict between student needs and faculty careers. Faculty teaching schedules (inelegantly called "loads") of three to four courses per year are expensive to maintain and usually are supported in large part by undergraduate student tuition and graduate teaching assistants. Research is important, and the education and training of graduate students is essential. However, the pursuit of these goals should not be subsidized by undergraduate students who pay high tuition but are then taught primarily by underpaid teaching assistants and other part-time faculty.

6. "Merit" scholarships are a major cost driver. In order to compete, universities and college provide merit aid unrelated to family income as an incentive for enrollment. They do this by raising the tuition for everyone and then discounting it for some. These funds do not come from endowments. Therefore, one measure to affect the cost structure of higher education would be to make "merit" financial aid taxable income for the recipient or the recipient's family. As merit aid is often related to academic qualifications as represented by SAT scores and high school class rank, and these variables are highly correlated to family income, some families are receiving more financial assistance than they "need" in order to pay for attendance. By making these funds taxable, we could encourage new ways of thinking about college as an investment in a student's future.

Reducing merit aid would also reduce the need for tuition discounting, so tuition overall could be reduced. Such a move would affect other forms of merit aid, including athletic awards. As most institutions are not highly selective, this could help level the competitive playing field. Tuition discounting also results in lower net tuition income, thus affecting faculty salaries and the quality of equipment and facilities. With tuition discounting at an average of 50 percent, and some institutions at 60 percent and more, some colleges are in jeopardy of financial failure.[8] Therefore, a reform of this practice could help institutions' financial status. After all, if a discount is the only reason students enroll, other changes need to be made.

These reforms, which come under the purview of board governance, could affect the cost of higher education to families and provide incentives for institutions to do more to control costs. Students and their success should come first in all considerations. Colleges and universities exist in order to teach students and help them become better prepared as citizens and professionals. Therefore, the board agenda should focus on student satisfaction, success, retention, and graduation, as well as on assistance for students in taking the next steps toward careers and graduate school.

What Should Universities Teach?

There is considerable evidence that many employers want graduates with particular skills, such as accounting, but the vast majority of employers also want employees with a broad set of skill and abilities, with an emphasis on effective oral and written communication, critical thinking and reasoning in multiple settings, and the ability to be imaginative across cultural borders. This form of preparation is valuable not only in training for critical reading, comprehensive listening, cogent writing, persuasive speaking, and proficiency in calculation, but also for asking questions. This kind of education needs to include general and expert knowledge, the skills just noted, abilities such as reasoning and a second language, and values such as respect for evidence, other opinions, and the balance of community and individual interests.

In addition to hard skills, students need also to develop soft skills, such as disciplined work habits, time management, teamwork, leadership, and community involvement through voluntarism. This development of hard and soft skills is a "liberating education," liberating students from their provincial upbringing, no matter their age, national origin, or station. Students also need to learn in context, whether through fieldwork, profession-based placements, or internships, each of which can help reinforce theory and an attitude of inquiry through practice.

One way to think about the question of what colleges should teach and what students should study is to reflect on contemporary crises in finance, industry, and politics, and ask what lessons have been learned. A quick survey of the past decade suggests that too many people, even those in sophisticated roles, lacked knowledge of history or historical analysis, and did not have the personal or professional memory in which to place contemporary issues.

History is an essential subject, especially if we are to understand the different ways people "know" the truth and how they challenge assumptions and validate assertions. In the study of history as defined here, we learn about the world we meet (nature or science); the world we make (culture); and the systems by which we mediate between them (law, morality, and ethics). We learn about the past and present, science and technology, war and peace, poetry and prose. We learn how we know what we think we know by learning to distinguish among empirical evidence, epiphanies or faith, and emotions based in fear or superstition.

The second area to develop is that of imagination. It seems clear in retrospect that high-profile people confronted new problems without the ability to see connections among different variables, visualize or forecast directions, or approach issues with creativity. They had not developed the capacity to inquire, to experience discovery, or to wonder, look, see, and ask. These are the benefits of an education that liberates students from prejudices masquerading as principles, no matter what their nationality, socioeconomic status, age, or religion. Students need to develop a global perspective even as they live, work, and volunteer locally.

The third area to develop is that of compassion. Many articles about leadership mention empathy (i.e., one's capacity to understand or experience the emotions of another) as necessary to lead others. While this is true, an educated person should also develop the capacity for compassion. If we move beyond sympathy (feeling sorry for another) and develop empathy (appreciating the pain or condition of another), then we can develop compassion, the ability to turn that empathy into action and to help another in need. This, too, is part of higher education's mission to prepare citizens and professionals.

Finally, college and university presidents should do more to tell the important story of higher education's benefits to society as well as to the individuals who live and vote in it. This form of risk management for the enterprise is as important as risk management for the campus. With good guidance, we can reclaim a culture of conscience and civic responsibility, of education for a purposeful life, for a university education that is as much or more about these goals than it is about jobs and economic development.

The measures outlined in this chapter are intended as investments for the security of a democratic society, not expenses to be added and cut as the political winds dictate. If we do not prepare our children to be ready for school; if our public schools are not prepared to ensure that all students are ready to learn; if our public schools, colleges, and universities are not adequately funded to fulfill their missions; if the federal government does not fund student aid adequately; if our academic leaders do not embrace a "liberating education" for all students; if our campus leaders do not support the central missions of our institutions and advocate for the support of student learning for life, not just for earning a living, we will further blunt these central instruments of democracy and witness the further decline of our nation.

Building a Brilliant Board

Many challenges to institutional governance are from external pressures, as previously noted. However, some challenges are generated internally, including from the board itself and its relationship with the president and the office of president. To be a successful board, the members must be well informed and exhibit trust in their relations with each other, loyalty to the mission and well-being of the institution, and civility in their relations with faculty, staff, students, and the community.

The role of the board is to think long term, to protect the institution's future from the actions of the present, since the pressures of the moment can cause administrators, including presidents, to focus on short-term demands. The presence of the board should make a difference in the prospects as well as the prosperity of the institution. Board members should act based on an inner conscience that underscores integrity, or at least act in response to an inner voice that warns that someone may be looking—that a certain action would not look good on the front page of the local paper.

Effective board members know or learn about the mission, purpose, and heritage of universities and bring questions rather than prescriptions to their deliberations. They seek to align the institution's reward structure with effective execution of its strategies for achieving the goals of student success and graduation.

Presidents face similar challenges. The temptations to act as if fundraising is divorced from student learning and faculty teaching are great. The pressures of fundraising, finance, and politics can lead a president to think of him- or herself as a corporate-style chief executive officer. Instead, the university needs a president who is the chief education officer, who chairs faculty meetings; reminds faculty, staff, and students of the purpose and heritage of the institution; and sees the top priority as enhancing the environment for teaching and learning.

Among the trustees' most important duties are ensuring adherence to the mission of the campus, assuring academic quality, and supporting strong presidential leadership. These are among some of the reasons that well-selected, well-trained trustees are essential to the success of American higher education. To quote author Marilynne Robinson, "We need only to allow the spread of learning to see the potential brilliance of humankind."[9]

Exercises and templates are included in the appendixes to assist boards in the orientation of new members and to guide current trustees, presidents, and others in campus leadership. We hope you find these illustrative examples helpful for building effective, strategic, and innovative processes of governance so that institutions of higher education may continue to grow and to thrive.

Exercises

- Ask to have the following questions put on the next board meeting agenda: (1) What are the top three external challenges we face? (2) What are the top three internal challenges we face? (3) What is our timeline for addressing each of these challenges?
- Engage a campus scholar who knows the institution's or campus's history and invite him or her to describe periods of significant change in the past. Then have the board discuss the relevance to contemporary challenges.
- Ask the head of the theater department to review the campus grounds and buildings as a stage set, with the mission statement and strategic plan goals as the story line, and to give the board a tour focusing on where and how the story line is supported and where it is blocked.
- Have the board and president discuss what would be different in terms of governance and priorities if the board did not exist, or if it existed but did not meet.
- Review the Decision, Discussion, and Information item templates discussed in Chapter 4. Discuss the purpose of each and the importance of the elements of each, such as alternatives and implications. Explore the topics of student satisfaction, success, retention, and graduation using each template.
- Engage the president in a discussion about his or her long-range aspirations and plans.
- Review model performance review templates for the board and board chair, with particular attention to how each template

encourages broadly based board participation and the avoidance of micromanagement.

- Develop a protocol for a change in presidential leadership, including the six months when an incoming president is learning about the institution and staff while the departing president is still serving as the chief executive officer.
- Schedule a board retreat for which the major agenda item is the future of the institution and how it will look in ten years in terms of curricula, students, faculty, staff, rewards, facilities, and technology.

Appendix A
Performance Review of the President

The board should submit a written review for each of these attributes, using examples when possible.

Basics: Understands the expectations of the role

Leadership Qualities: Initiative/self-starter; team player; gains respect and cooperation; is responsive; engages in self-assessment; has a positive effect on institutional culture; able to communicate effectively on and off campus

Personal Qualities: Integrity; positive presentation in public

Judgment and Sensitivity: Acknowledges others; challenges, motivates, evaluates, and rewards others; makes timely and sound decisions

Knowledge and Skills: Demonstrates knowledge and skills through planning and execution; prudent steward of institutional assets; anticipates trends and develops timely responses; follows up appropriately on special board task forces

Board Relations: Works well with all members; communicates well with the board; keeps board, especially the chair, apprised of important issues

Senior Staff Relations: Selection and assessment of senior staff; development of senior staff; plan for succession and talent management

Faculty-Staff Relations: Good rapport with campus constituents; effective communications with campus constituents

Community Relations: Represents the institution well; promotes the mission effectively; has respect of peers; effective communicator

Future Goals: Fulfills responsibilities for the achievement of selected goals, including enrollment, financial stability, retention and graduation rates, accreditation and quality assurances, etc.

Strength and Development Needs: Major strengths; opportunities for development

Overall appraisal:

Signed_____ Date_____

Appendix B
Orientation Packet

All new trustees should be given a packet of materials that includes at least the following information:

- A history of the institution, so that the new trustee is aware of the heritage and purpose that inform the board's deliberations
- The charter and bylaws, because colleges and universities are legal entities whose public purpose is authorized by a state charter and whose board operations are guided by a set of bylaws
- A memorandum on the duties and expectations of trustees that should reference attendance, preparation, speaking up and asking questions, being collegial with other members and the president, participation at campus events such as the beginning of the school year and commencement, committing the time and talent to support and represent the campus, knowing the difference between governance and management, being committed to the board mentoring program, and making donations to the annual fund, capital campaigns, and special occasions such as an annual gala to raise funds for scholarships
- The most recent strategic plan, including goals, strategies, assumptions, milestones for monitoring progress, results to date, and the allocation of responsibilities
- An organizational chart indicating the institution's officers and direct reports, with solid and dotted lines showing the various reporting relationships

- The latest financial report, external audit, and audit firm's management letter indicating the institution's fiscal health for the past year in comparison to the previous year, including any unusual fiscal or debt practices
- The most recent report from a bond-rating agency
- The most recent tax return and explanations of any comments or sanctions
- A copy of the board's compensation policies for the president and senior officers, with compensation history
- The book or directory of historical and comparative academic, enrollment, financial, and facilities data, including information about student graduation rates, student debt upon graduation, loan default rates, capital bonding levels and ratings, population characteristics for the regions served, etc.
- A copy of the D&O (directors and officers) liability insurance policy, institutional indemnification policy, and the codes of conduct applying to trustees, officers, faculty, staff, students, and vendors, etc.
- An assessment of potential liabilities that might result from vendors, employees, students, government entities, and clinical service recipients, etc.
- Brief biographical sketches, photographs, contact information, and descriptions of the responsibilities of the vice presidents, deans, and other senior staff members who attend board meetings
- A sample agenda for each committee and the full board illustrating decision, discussion, and information items
- Minutes of committee and full board meetings for the previous year
- A copy of the president's confidential periodic report distributed to the board before each meeting or on some other regular schedule
- A list of committees and members
- A calendar of the year's meetings and occasions when trustees are expected to be present
- A handbook with definitions of terms and policies about items such as tenure, sabbatical, and shared governance
- A description of the process for preparing meeting agendas

- A description by the president of his or her approach to leadership and management and the top three to five issues of greatest concern to the senior staff
- A roster of collaborations with other institutions and community organizations

In addition, the packet and the ensuing orientation discussion should include the following:

- A roster of the state and national organizations in which the institution and its officers hold membership, and the purpose and dues for each
- Information about board expense reimbursement for travel and lodging relative to attendance at board meetings and campus events
- Regional, state, and national professional development meetings and conferences for trustees, such as the AGB annual meeting, and samples of reading materials that will be sent between meetings (including the Association of Governing Board's *Trusteeship* magazine, the weekly edition of *The Chronicle of Higher Education*, and links to online access to the daily *Inside Higher Education* e-newsletter)
- Any other pertinent information

Appendix C

Bylaws

The guide to a board's operations are the bylaws, including descriptions of the role and scope of each committee. Bylaws cover the following topics:

Article I: Name of institution.

Article II: Purpose as stated in the state-granted charter.

Article III: Membership, including the minimum and maximum number of trustees, the length and number of terms, and both general and specific expectations of members.

Article IV: Officers and elections, including names of offices, system of nominations and elections, criteria for eligibility, terms of office, board chair's role and responsibilities between meetings, and how to deal with vacancies and removal from office.

Article V: Meetings, including regular meetings, special meetings, notices of meetings, and quorum requirements.

Article VI: Committees, including a charter for each, the minimum number of members, expertise needed, the meeting schedule, eligibility for ex officio status, limits on committee authority, and the process for appointing special or additional committees.

Article VII: Finances, including a definition of the fiscal year; the process for adopting a budget; and descriptions of internal controls, audit protocols, investment policies, and the process for reviewing tax forms, etc.

Article VIII: Parliamentary authority, usually *Robert's Rules of Order.*

Article IX: Amendments, including the timing of notice for proposed amendments and methods of voting.

Article X: Conflict of Interest Policy, including definitions of "interested party" and "financial interest," procedures for disclosing and addressing real and potential conflicts of interest, and procedures for the annual review of potential conflicts, as well as a draft of the form regarding real and potential conflicts to be filed each year by each member and the president.

Appendix D

Board Meeting Agenda

One way to organize the full board's agenda for a meeting is to arrange the sections as follows:

Roll call.

Approval of the minutes of the previous meeting.

Motion to enter executive session; all but trustees and president leave, unless otherwise specified.

Approval of the minutes of the previous executive session.

Board chair's comments.

Confidential president's report; Q&A about the president's confidential periodic report or any other topic.

President leaves the executive session.

Trustees meet in executive session alone or with selected advisors, perhaps legal counsel or auditors.

Motion to exit executive session; all are invited back into the meeting.

Board chair's comments.

President's report for the open session.

Decision items in sequence by committee, starting with any consent agenda items.

A special discussion item, such as a report from a dean, a discussion of a proposed building project, or an update on the strategic plan.

Discussion items in sequence by committee.

Information items in sequence by committee.

Dates of future meetings.

Appendix E

Confidential Periodic Report of the President

This Confidential Memorandum is a template including illustrative examples from real-life campus operations.

CONFIDENTIAL MEMORANDUM

To: Board of Trustees

From: [name], President

Date: [date]

Re: Confidential Periodic Report

I.   *Board Business*

We held a special orientation session for [name] on [date].

Each June, we review the Bylaws of the full Board and the committees of the Board. Please review the Bylaws in the Board Book.

The Board Self-Evaluation Survey included in the Board Book will be summarized and discussed at our meeting.

You may recall that [name] suggested at the last Finance Committee meeting and at the full Board meeting that we convene a special task force to consider goals and strategies for tuition pricing. I have drafted a charge, possible membership, and timeline that I have reviewed with the officers and included in the Board Book. We will discuss this at the meeting on [date].

We will distribute the new roster of Committee chairs and members.

As part of my Annual Report, I will provide a summary of the past year in terms of highlights, goals and challenges met, and continuing concerns.

I also will present an updated approach to succession planning for each of the senior officers.

II.   *Committee Agenda Summaries*

   A. Academic Affairs
     The principal agenda items are *personnel decisions* and *proposed degree programs.* The Provost and I will give an *update on the School of Business,* its Interim Dean search, the role of the expanded cabinet in the School, and *AACSB status.*

   B. Advancement
     The Committee will hear a report on the *success of the Scholarship Gala* and the *status of assessing the Comprehensive Campaign.*

   C. Audit
     The major topic will be a *presentation on Enterprise Risk Management,* which will include our insurance broker, audit firm, and legal counsel. This discussion will be summarized for the full Board.

   D. Buildings & Grounds
     At the last meeting of the Committee, and at the full Board meeting, [name] suggested that we inquire into the possibility of acquiring an *interest-rate lock.* Staff will brief the Finance Committee on this. Our advisors are suggesting that we wait a year. We don't need to borrow money for new construction until [date], so if we were to borrow on a "forward delivery" in [date], with delivery

in [date], we could lock in the interest rates. The CFO will explain the costs and consequences of this.

E. Executive Committee
The Executive Committee *met to approve candidates for May degrees.*

F. Finance and Administration
Major topics will include *an updated contract review policy* and *consideration of the role of the endowment and the use of unrestricted investment income.*

Following this, the Committee will *meet in joint session* with the Student Life Committee.

G. Investment
The Investment Committee will report on and *recommend changes in the contract review policy in order to allow it to change fund managers up to a certain dollar limit on an investment without full Board approval.*

H. Student Life
The *Committee will meet on its own and in combination with the Finance Committee.* In each case it will *discuss enrollment, student financial aid, admission yield rates, retention,* the results *of the three financial aid pilot programs,* and *ideas about how to make these pilots sustainable.*

We also will discuss *how we counsel students about borrowing and debt. See Attachment "A" for information made available to student borrowers.*

At the last meeting, [name] asked about the potential benefits of *guaranteeing a four-year rate for tuition.* We already allow people to pay four years in advance at the current rate, but *do not guarantee the rate for four years to others.* This plan has generally not worked elsewhere because it *ignores the potential effects of inflation and drops in enrollment on future revenue.*

However, [University] *is introducing* a *"tuition lock"* which includes a significant increase in tuition over the current rate, and $8,000 a year more per student than our tuition rate.

We have had much *less* overlap *in scholarship offers with* [University] this year. We wonder if it is allocating more of its financial aid to students from outside the region so as to increase that enrollment in order to fill empty dormitory beds.

I. Trustee Affairs
The Trustee Affairs Committee *will recommend the Slate of Officers, the Slate of Board Members for re-election, and a special exception to the Bylaws to elect former trustee [name] as Trustee Emeritus.*

III. *Continuing and Emerging Concerns*

A. Student Loans
There have been *many articles about student debt, student loans, and the relationship* of the availability of debt *to increases in tuition and* alleged *excessive facilities development on campuses*. It is important to keep in mind that some of the examples cited in the press are anomalies. There is no reason, other than personal choice, for someone to graduate from [University] with $120,000 in debt. The *New York Times* misspoke when it talked about the average amount of debt. In fact, the average amount of student debt is approximately $25,000 per year. We are right in the middle, and that includes debt from those who attend the state university campuses.

One of the problems is that the federal government allows students and families to borrow the maximum amounts in the loan programs, even if that amount far exceeds the bill for tuition and fees. In fact, *we have employees who receive tuition remission and still borrow the maximum amount. We have students who borrow at the maximum amount and then get refunds because the loan amount exceeds the tuition and fees.*

The great debate about allowing the interest rate to rise to 6.8 percent from 3.4 percent is out of proportion to the problem of student debt. The change is a prospective action which affects only one small part of college loans. The *major problems are with federal limits untied to financial "need," so-called alternative loans that charge 12 percent and up in interest rates per year, and predatory for-profit colleges that result in both high debt loads and high default rates.*

There have been some good articles about higher education and finance. I include a *report from Moody's Investor Services* that was presented at the CICU (Commission on Independent Colleges and Universities) Annual Meeting. It is a *"check-up" on fiscal indicators and market dynamics* (see Attachment "B"). Another article is entitled "Three Dangerous Student Aid Myths," from the journal *University Business*, the magazine of the National Association of Collegiate Business Officers (see Attachment "C").

A related issue is the *fees charged for student use of debit and prepaid cards.* We do not do this.

A recent report from Eduventures indicates the *high correlation between student matriculation and the quality of academic facilities,* countering the myth that students are attracted by "climbing walls" and "near-spa" experiences.

B. Leadership Development
Thank you again for your support of Vice President [name] entering the executive doctoral program.

We are delighted to report that [name] *will be joining us as Interim Dean of the School of Business.*

It is hard to imagine, but *Deans [name] and [name] have been with us almost a year.* They have made such an impact that they are already central to life on campus.

I have held *several meetings with the School of Business Cabinet, consisting of administrators and faculty, with Senior*

Associate Provost [name] installed as co-chair. I think we are making good progress in the school.

C. Advertising/Marketing
I have decided to engage [name] Communications to assess our advertising and marketing activities. As we have an in-house advertising agency, thus saving fees, we do not have the benefit of comparative analysis through an RFP with other firms. I also think we may put too much investment in "image" advertising and not enough into program-specific "action advertising" for academic programs and locations. I will report on the results.

D. Athletics
As I indicated at an earlier point, *we will move Men's Soccer to Division II so that all sports will be part of Division II in the [name] Conference.*

E. *ELS*
We will have a *special Information Item on the relationship between us and ELS (English Language Services) of Berlitz.* This is a long-standing partnership that not only is successful in terms of net revenue to the University, but also in adding international diversity to the campus through guest and matriculated students. *I think you will find the information of great interest.*

F. *On-Line Learning and Implications*
As a follow-up to the discussions about technology and learning at the Academic Affairs Committee, we will present an overview of on-line learning opportunities, challenges, and implications. (This will be sent under separate cover.)

IV. *Finances*

The CFO gave a presentation on finances at the full faculty meeting so that everyone knows the financial condition of the University. I frequently remind faculty and staff that "enrollment is everyone's job, if everyone is to have a job," and underscore the importance of student satisfaction and success to future enrollment as well as to institutional recognition.

V.   *Alumni/Fundraising Activities*

The weekend of [date] will include reunion by alumni of all ages with many activities. The Friday evening dinner for "young alumni" will have almost 300 in attendance. Saturday afternoon will include a special program for members of the *Academy of Distinction,* with about 80 expected. *Several trustees will be speaking* as part of the ceremony. The Saturday evening events will host over 200. Nearly 100 returnees are staying in residence halls.

The 50th Reunion Class attended Commencement.

We held the *Scholarship Reception,* which is always well attended, and a *new School of Business reception initiated by two faculty members who have created endowments for scholarships.*

The *Parents Association* held an active meeting and the *Athletic Hall of Fame dinner was another sell-out.*

The *Wall Street Networking Event was successful.* The *President's Advisory Group* met at [name] Corporation. The event was hosted by an alumna who is one of the most senior women at the corporation.

The President's Scholarship Gala was a great success again this year.

Former Trustee [name] visited campus for several days to discuss his endowed *Summer Scholars Program,* which is off to a great start.

Alumnus [name(s)] visited campus for a day, meeting with deans and the advancement staff and speaking briefly at the full Faculty meeting about what he will say as *the Matriculation Day speaker in August.*

More than 50 percent of the Honors College Class of [date] made a gift to the Honors College Scholarship Endowment!

We have received several new gifts, including one from an *area developer to endow scholarships for students in public health.*

Vice President [name] will *present an overview on corporate and foundation gifts in response to a request from the Committee.* He also will report on the *search for a new Executive Director of Alumni Relations.*

As a *surprise* at lunch during the board meeting, we will announce that the Alumni Council has *elected Dean [name] as an honorary alumnus.*

We hosted a dinner for alumni and friends in the *insurance industry* in order to learn about opportunities for our students. *Trustee [name] was especially helpful in organizing the gathering.* We have held similar dinners for alumni and friends in other industries for similar reasons.

VI. *Administrative/Legal/Labor Issues*

We will undertake an *assessment of Greek Life during the coming months.* There is no problem at the present time, but we want to ensure that we have the best programs we can.

We debriefed after the court decision on the Virginia Polytechnic Institute case. Even though the case was dismissed, there are lessons to be learned.

We were *visited by a Board member of X College* to see if we might be interested in entering into some form of strategic alliance or partnership with the College, which is facing great difficulty. I am not interested in their debt or deferred maintenance, but am interested in some of their students.

Due to changes in federal healthcare regulations regarding *student health insurance,* insurance premiums are projected to increase dramatically. We are doing what we can to understand and control these costs.

A federal bankruptcy judge ruled that a student (not here) with Asperger's Syndrome could discharge her federal loan obligations of nearly $340,000 because her disorder qualifies her for a federal exemption. This ruling could have significant ramifications on all institutions.

The Provost and I *met with the School of Education Advisory Council, as we do with each of the unit advisory boards from time-to-time.*

We engaged *outside reviewers for University College,* our unit for adult students, and the reviewers gave some good suggestions as to what we might do to improve services. We engage outside reviewers for all programs on a periodic basis.

Long-time Associate Dean [name] is retiring, and a wonderful celebration was held in his honor at Chelsea Piers. Both Trustees [name] and [name] attended.

The Provost and I hosted two receptions at the President's House for accepted students and their parents.

We held the *Annual Employee Recognition Dinner,* honoring those who have been here ten, fifteen, twenty, twenty-five, thirty, *and over forty years.*

Professor [name], President of the local AAUP, asked me to meet with a group of her AAUP colleagues from around the state at a meeting she was hosting on campus. I was happy to meet with them to discuss higher education issues.

VII. *Campus Climate*

The International Student Reception held after Commencement hosted over 180 students and parents.

We have a new *association of Chinese students and scholars,* which invited me to speak at its inaugural luncheon about a week after I returned from China.

We *hosted the Orpheus Chamber Orchestra on campus as* part of our continuing music series.

The end of the semester brought customary events for Nurse Pinning, late-night breakfast during finals, and *an extraordinary Commencement exercise.*

The *dates for Commencement next year* are as follows: Doctoral Hooding—[date]; Commencement Dinner—[date]; and the 117th Commencement Ceremony—[date]. *We would like to have more Trustees in attendance than we did this year.*

VIII. *Federal Relations*

U.S. Senator [name] visited campus to host a news conference on federal support for veterans programs, in which we are already active, and then had lunch with several of us, including some trustees.

Congress Member [name] was on campus for this event and again for the Annual Congressional Art Competition.

IX. *State Relations*

We continue to be *active with* the *cIcu in Albany* and talk with our local legislators there and locally, including at events such as the Memorial Day Parade.

X. *Regional Relations*

We held a *ribbon cutting at our new nursing facilities at the Medical Center connected with* the hospital near to our Dutchess County facility.

I continue to be *active with the Regional Chamber as a member of the Board, the Executive Committee, and the Finance Committee.*

XI. *Village Relations*

I mentioned Memorial Day. We also hosted the annual meeting to decide on the next round of *The Prize for Leadership winners,* something I do in conjunction with the Village Administrator and School District Superintendent. Winners are not limited to the local public high school. The ten prizes are open to any local resident who is a junior in high school, no matter where he or she goes to school. We typically have three to four high schools represented.

Several of us attended the annual *Gala of the Village Chamber of Commerce,* at which a member of our Center for Health Innovation Advisory Board was honored.

XII. *Special Accomplishments of Faculty, Staff, and Students*

[Name] won the First-Year Student Award.

Professor [name] was elected to the National Collegiate Hispanic Honor Society for his life-long commitment to Spanish language and literature.

A number of our *students have been admitted to prestigious law schools,* along with doctoral programs and medical schools. [Name], President of the Student Government Association, will be going to *[University]* with a significant scholarship, and [name] will attend *[University].* Others were admitted to *equally prestigious institutions.*

The magazines *Erudition* and *Catalyst* are out, and we are receiving positive comments about them.

The *University won another Conference Championship in the EPA Green Power Challenge,* a voluntary program encouraging institutions to buy green power. We won by *off-setting 100 percent of our electrical load by purchasing over twenty million kilowatt hours of renewable energy credits through a private company.*

Two students received Fulbright Awards for next year.

Our institution was again given top *reviews by* The Princeton Review's *Guide to Green Colleges*.

Student [name] won recognition as the Conference Tennis "Player of the Year."

Professor [name] was elected Conference Committee Chair and Board Vice President of the Association of Writers and Writing Programs.

Student [name] was recognized by the Public Relations Professionals of Long Island with a scholarship awarded at the association's annual gala.

The *Annual Brown and Gold Banquet* of the Student Government Association and Center for Student Involvement was another great success, with awards distributed to student leaders.

XIII. *Professional Activities*

The day after returning from China, I was Keynote Speaker and "Man of the Year" Honoree at the ASIS International Long Island Chapter.

A few days after that, I *led a program on governance at the Association of Governing Boards annual meeting in Washington, DC.*

I participated on the *Committee on Economic Development study on postsecondary opportunities, which has been published.*

While in China, a member of the Admissions staff and I gave two presentations in Shanghai and two in Beijing. *The first in each city* consisted of a video, a PowerPoint presentation, and a presentation and Q&A led by me for fifty-plus agents who specialize in counseling Chinese families about higher education in the United States. *The second session in each city* was for the parents of current students, prospective students and parents, and a few others. We had hoped to meet some alumni, but most of our graduates live outside the areas of Shanghai and Beijing.

The trip was *sponsored by ELS* and was of assistance to them as they recruit and screen students to gain English proficiency here before becoming applicants to U.S. colleges.

In addition to Shanghai and Beijing, we visited Xi'an, where I took photographs for a new exhibit.

XIV. *Conclusion*

Thank you for all that you do for our institution. See you soon.

Attachments

A. Consumer Awareness Notification Points for Student Borrowers

B. Moody's "Outlook for Higher Education"

C. "Three Dangerous Student Aid Myths"

Appendix F
Dean's Report

Academic unit:

Dean:

Years at _____University:

Bio ....(Attachment "A")
I.   Profile .... (Attachment "B")
    (Vision for unit; faculty, by rank and years at the institution;
    enrollment by degree level and location; facilities and space use;
    4-year financial analysis)

II.   Academic Programs by Degree Level and Location
    ....(Attachment "C")

III.   Scholarly and Creative Interests of the Faculty
    ....(Attachment "D")

IV.   Quality Measures ....(Attachment "E")
    (Accreditation, other)

V.   Postgraduate Placement of Students........... (Attachment "F")

VI.   National Trends; State and Federal Regulatory Issues
    ....(Attachment "G")

VII.   Goals: 1-3 years ....(Attachment "H")
    (Enrollment, staffing, facilities/space, academic programs, field
    placements, etc.)

VIII.   Special Opportunities....................................(Attachment "I")
    (Alumni relations, grants, fundraising, etc.)

Appendix G

Transition Memorandum

MEMORANDUM

TO: [name], President-Elect

FROM: [name], President

DATE: [date]

RE: Thoughts on the Transition

Personnel Matters

I am preparing brief performance reviews of the vice presidents and will give them to you before the week is out.

As I hope you know, the Provost, CFO, chief development officer, and assistant secretary to the board are superior performers in all that they do.

The vice president for Communications (VPC) is doing well in her reduced portfolio and is an essential aide in campus, eternal community, and crisis communications.

While the vice president for Enrollment Management (VPEM) has a large portfolio, Athletics, Public Safety, and Student Life have strong leaders who need little direct guidance. In addition, many presidents have Athletics report to them. I do not agree with this.

The staffs in Admissions and Student Financial Services are very strong. An area of concern is the relationship between Enrollment Management and those who should be key partners, like the deans and Provost's staff. I will say more about this when we talk. For further commentary, see my memo on succession planning to the board for the [date] meeting.

Both the Senior Associate Provost (SAP) and the Senior Advisor for Facilities (SAF) meet with the senior staff and are valuable participants in all discussions. The SAP is a terrific thinker, writer, and statistician, a rare combination. The SAF is a quiet but extremely knowledgeable and experienced officer with vast understanding of admissions and facilities, and expert sensitivities when it comes to Village communications.

As the Internal Auditor has just started, I will prepare a rather thin review for her, but will use the format I have used for reviewing the previous occupant of this position.

Policy Concerns

There are several areas related to undergraduate admissions that deserve consideration, including changing the emphasis on SAT scores in admissions and financial aid, and making a change in how we use General Studies, our program for students who do not fully meet admissions standards. (See the background material prepared for the last board meeting.)

In addition, I think we should treat Trustees as "prospects," inviting them to speak on campus, participate in the COACH (Count on Alumni for Career Help) and related programs more regularly, and in other ways encourage their philanthropy by broadening the ways in which they engage with the campus. I think this can be done without violating a fundamental principle guiding the board's role—"noses in, fingers out"—so as not to confuse governance and management roles. We could do more to involve trustees as we would other prospects without breaching this wall.

Prospects

There are a number of individuals with whom I have strong relationships, some of whom I call regularly and with whom we have been discussing potential new gifts of various types and sizes. These include [a list of two dozen people followed]:

Please let me know how you wish to discuss the prospects, potential proposals, and follow up.

Consultants
I have asked the VPEM to bring in our advertising and marketing vendors in order to hear about their progress in fulfilling the assignments we have given them. I also have asked my assistant to organize a meeting with our public relations firm to do the same.

Community Leaders
Due to your change in schedule, I will not be able to introduce you to the Mayor and Village Administrator, the leader of the local Property Owner's Association, the president of the Regional Chamber, the head of our public relations firm, or other elected officials. In most cases, the VPC can introduce you.

Conclusion
While I will be on sabbatical effective this June, I will of course be available for your questions.

I wish you well. This is a great place, with a distinctive character and a wonderful future. Enjoy it.

Appendix H

Model Succession Planning Memorandum

MODEL SUCCESSION PLANNING MEMORANDUM
CONFIDENTIAL DRAFT—FOR BOARD DISCUSSION
ONLY—DO NOT DISTRIBUTE

[date]

Subject: Succession Planning, Talent Management, and Professional Development

Background
It is prudent to establish succession plans, talent management priorities, and professional development strategies for key staff as an ongoing priority in order to prepare for known retirements and unanticipated departures. We have an ongoing process of professional development for the senior staff and deans, which involves special assignments, readings, conferences, consultants, retreats, and discussions of "what if?" as well as active involvement in the broader community by serving on boards, etc. We also have encouraged advanced study and writing.

It is best to present some dimensions of these plans orally, rather than put them on paper, given the sensitive nature of such discussions.

I subscribe to what is termed the 70-20-10 Rule for professional development: 70 percent of training is from challenging assignments; 20 percent is from developmental relationships; and 10 percent is from coursework and training sessions.

I had suggested to the Chair that the Board should engage a search consultant to help the Board and the campus community assess what experiences, characteristics, and competencies are desired in the next president. This phase would be followed by a broad-based search to find a person with the characteristics desired.

During this period, the Board also should consider how best to utilize the knowledge, relationships, experiences, and other strengths of the future President Emeritus in achieving ongoing academic, executive, and fundraising goals.

Professional development considerations and succession planning for the President are as follows:
I view involvement in meetings with, and especially through readings sponsored by cIcu (the Commission on Independent Colleges and Universities of New York), the American Council on Education (ACE), the American Association of Colleges and Universities (AAC&U), the Association of Governing Boards (AGB), and the National Association of Independent Colleges and Universities (NAICU) as professional development, due to the programs and publications sponsored and the opportunities for leadership among peers.

In addition, participation on boards, writing for publication, my television program, and my art exhibits, etc., are other forms of professional development opportunities for me, as they challenge my mind and talents, and they are occasions to represent the University.

I provide opportunities for the Provost to learn all aspects of the University, so as to be able to "step in" if needed as acting president. I do this by including her in various meetings of Board Committees, such as Audit, B&G, Finance and Administration, and Investment, in addition to the expected committees of Academic Affairs and Student Life, as well as alumni and fund-raising activities.

For example, the Provost serves as the University's representative for the Society that recognizes those who donate $1,000 or more each year, and is also called upon to represent the University at various events. These are areas in which she continues to show great promise. The Provost also attends conferences with select national groups, such as ACE and AAC&U.

Professional development considerations and succession planning for the Provost are as follows:
The Provost is being prepared to serve as president when needed. See above.

If a successor were needed for the Provost, we could appoint as Acting Provost a dean with appropriate experience before undertaking a national search. At the moment, the dean with such experience overall is Dr. [name]. We are helping him become familiar with the University beyond his role as dean, including the institution at large, external relations, and the role of Provost, through various forms of development. We have made sure that he is exposed to the Board. He has been a dean before so this is not unknown territory for him.

Professional development considerations and succession planning for the CFO are as follows:
The CFO engages in ongoing CPA professional development, as well as seminars on investment and legal matters. He manages our risk-management issues and teaches in an investment class. We also engage him in fundraising strategy and select visits with prospective donors.

If the CFO had the academic credentials, he could perform any duty in the University. As it is, he can do all but the academic. I have been encouraging him to burnish his academic credentials by teaching in our investment classes, among others. We encourage him to attend seminars, write for bulletins and journals, and speak at conferences. He is the "go-to" person; I give him numerous special assignments related to strategic and Board issues, and he performs extremely well.

If a successor to the CFO were needed, the Associate Vice President for Finance and Controller could assume the duties of Treasurer for at least an interim period.

For the Associate Vice President (AVP), the major professional development goal is to become familiar with all financial areas reporting to the CFO, which we are doing, and to become known to the Board. He is doing well and has the confidence of his peers and the senior staff.

The other areas for which the CFO is responsible, Human Resources, Labor Relations, Legal, Risk Management, Investments, Debt issuance, and relations with investment bankers, are outside the range of the AVP's strengths and interest. Therefore, we would need to look externally for one or more persons to oversee these areas. (It should be noted again that a neighboring university has three vice presidents doing what our CFO does on his own.)

If the CFO were to leave, we could create the position of CFO with the same portfolio or divide up his responsibilities. For example, the new CFO could be responsible for treasury and controller functions, investments, debt issuance and relations with investment banks. However, human resources, labor relations, and risk management could be assigned to a new vice presidential role.

Even if the CFO remains, which we hope he will do, we still would need to create a position to assume the functions of the departing Senior Advisor for Facilities (and former vice president for Administration and Student Services), who has been overseeing both facilities and construction. This new position could include administration as well as facilities and construction, and, if needed, human resources, labor relation, and legal.

Nevertheless, with the increasing emphasis on Title IX cases and our appointment of a lawyer as Title IX coordinator, we may be approaching the point when in-house counsel would be required. I will examine this need again this year.

Professional development considerations and succession planning for Vice President for University Advancement are as follows:
The Vice President for University Advancement (VPUA) works closely with me and our campaign consultant, who, together with me, serves as an advisor-tutor-mentor for him. The CFO also assists. I have urged the VPUA to write for professional journals and to complete a doctoral program, which he has done.

If a successor for the VPUA were needed, either one of his direct reports could assume the role on at least an interim basis of up to one year. The VPUA and I regularly discuss the professional development needs of his staff and provide opportunities for growth and training for them through assignments and training.

Professional development considerations and succession planning for Vice President for Communications are as follows:
The VP for Communications (VPC) attends professional seminars covering her areas of responsibility, including emergency and crisis communications. These are areas of significant need for this position, she enjoys them, and she is doing well in them. I also give her special assignments in crisis communications, foster her working relationship with Public Safety, and will provide her opportunities to be involved in fundraising.

Effective this July, I will transfer to Enrollment Management all advertising, marketing, and social media responsibilities that are related to admissions.

If the VPC were to leave, I would create a vice president for public relations position focused entirely on general and emergency communications with the various constituents and media on and off campus. Depending upon the candidate selected, I would consider transferring Community Relations to the President and publications and government relations to the VPUA, where they are located at many other universities.

The highest priorities for professional development in Communications are to continue to prepare back-ups for those responsible for media and public relations, publications, and community relations.

Professional development considerations and succession planning for the Vice President for Enrollment Management and Student Success.
We hired the Vice President for Enrollment Management and Student Success (VPEMSS) effective [date] last year.

Enrollment management includes all admissions, student financial services, and off-campus administration. The head of Student Financial Services is Assistant Vice President [name] and the head of Admissions is Assistant Vice President [name]. Both are highly accomplished, especially in undergraduate admissions. Back-ups for them are being trained.

Student Success includes the Center for Student Involvement, Career Development and Internships, Residential Life and Housing, Commuter Student Services, Health Services Center, Interfaith Center, Auxiliary Services (the University Center and University Dining Services), Cultural Affairs, International Student Services, New Student Orientation, Student Conduct and Community Standards, Disability Support Services, Student Government Association, and Student Counseling Center. [Name] continues as Associate Vice President overseeing these areas as well as serving as liaison to the deans for adult and graduate enrollment under the VPEMSS's supervision. The head of Public Safety and Campus Transportation also reports to the Vice President for Enrollment Management and Student Success.

We have successfully completed the search for a new Athletic Director (AD). The AD also reports to the Vice President for Enrollment Management and Student Success.

The foregoing offices are the ones most directly related to student out-of-class experiences and therefore must, in my opinion, be coordinated for student satisfaction and success.

I discuss the professional development needs of this staff and herself routinely with the VPEMSS.

Professional development considerations and succession planning for the Senior Advisor for Facilities are as follows: The Senior Advisor for Facilities scaled back on his responsibilities as Vice President for Administration and Student Services effective March 1. He is focusing on facilities, especially Facilities Plan Phase I design and construction , as well as facility renovations.

Facilities Management is headed by an experienced Executive Director who plans to retire in 15 months. The Senior Advisor for Facilities will continue to supervise Facilities Management through Phase I, including the remainder of the next year. When the Executive Director officially announces his retirement this fall, we will search for a successor.

In anticipation of the Senior Advisor's retirement, we will consider the portfolio of duties and design a new position. However, the composition of duties will depend upon the CFO's plans.

If the CFO were to leave, we would need not only to hire a new CFO but also to consider whether we would need to hire an internal attorney to oversee some of what the CFO does now as well as what a new vice president for facilities management would do.

If the CFO stays, Facilities Management could report to him, especially if we have an Executor Director for Facilities Management as talented as the current one.

We have active programs of professional development for each of those named as well as for their direct reports.

Notes

Introduction. Why a Guide?

1. Greer, "Healthy Skepticism about Polls."
2. Lederman, "Number of College Faculty and Staff"; NCES Digest, tables 315.10, 333.90, 334.10, and 334.30.
3. June, "Adjuncts Build Strength."
4. Bowen, *Board Book*.
5. Jencks and Riesman, *Academic Revolution*.
6. Boyer, *Scholarship Reconsidered*.
7. Drucker, quoted in AGB, "Higher Education Must Change," 17.

Chapter 1. Historical and Structural Framework of Governance

1. Harvard College, "Mission, Vision, and History."
2. Wellesley College, "Wellesley's Mission."
3. Horace Webster, quoted in CCNY, "About: Our History."
4. Carlson, "When College Was a Public Good."
5. Lederman, "Number of Colleges and Universities Drops Sharply."
6. Oliff et al., "Recent Deep State Higher Education Cuts."
7. Schrecker, "Bad Old Days."
8. Kirkpatrick, *Rise of Non-Resident Government*.
9. Cole, *Great American University*.

Chapter 2. Board Responsibilities

1. Legon, "10 Habits."
2. Kerr and Gade, *Guardians*.
3. AGB, *Policies, Practices, and Composition*.
4. AGB, *Effective Governing Boards*.
5. MSCHE, *Standards for Accreditation*, 13th ed.

6. Jaschik, "Pressure from All Sides."
7. NAICU, "College Board Releases 2016 Edition."
8. Jaschik, "Shocking Decision at Sweet Briar."
9. IIE, "Open Doors."
10. Jaschik, "Admissions Group Calls for Transparency"; Seltzer, "Small College Problems."
11. Redden, "Number of International Branch Campuses."
12. Eliot, *University Administration*, 37.
13. Stross, "Don't Blame Silicon Valley." See also Leuty, "Biggest Biotech"; Reingold, "Theranos' Board."
14. Foley, "To Fix Metro."
15. Deloitte Center, "Role of the Board."
16. Sonnenfeld, "What Makes Great Boards."
17. "Sweezy v. New Hampshire," *Law and Higher Education*.
18. CUNY, "Directory of U.S. Faculty Contracts."
19. Scott, "Revealing the Truth."
20. Carter, "Princeton Reaches $18M Settlement"; Mitchell, "Suffolk University and the Collapse."
21. Texas Public Policy Foundation, "'7 Solutions' Summary."
22. AGB, *Consequential Board Governance*.
23. Mitchell, "New Rules of Engagement."
24. "Evaluating the Board," *Chief Executive*; Regan, *Presidents and Board Chairs*.

Chapter 3. Board Membership

1. AGB, *Policies, Practices, and Composition*.
2. Mitchell, "New Rules of Engagement."
3. "Becoming a Successful Board Chair," *Board Forward*.
4. AGB, *Policies, Practices, and Composition*.
5. Callan and Honetschlager, *Policies for Improving Trustee Selection*.

Chapter 4. Processes and Procedures

1. Hampshire-Cowan, "Four Cs of Board Leadership."
2. Selingo, "Job Nobody Can Seem to Keep."
3. Carter, "Why Turnover Is Growing."
4. Carter, "Survey: Higher Ed in Crisis."
5. Selingo et al., "Pathways to University Presidency."

6. Carter, "What Makes a College President?"

7. Greer, *Prospective Governance.*

8. Machiavelli, *The Prince*, Chapter 23.

Chapter 5. Strategic Leadership

1. Chait, *Governance as Leadership.*

2. Greer, *Prospective Governance.*

3. Legon, "10 Habits."

4. BoardMax, "2015 Board Engagement Report."

5. Bennis and Thomas, "Crucibles of Leadership."

6. Kellerman, "Leadership."

7. Machiavelli, *The Prince*, Chapter 23.

Chapter 6. Leading Higher Education into the Future

1. Riddell, "Data Shows Decade's Dramatic Shift."

2. Lumina Foundation, *Strategic Plan.*

3. Seltzer, "Private Colleges and Universities Increase Tuition Discounting."

4. Institute for College Access and Success, "Quick Facts about Student Debt."

5. Scott, "Modern American University."

6. Scott, "Modern American University," 7.

7. National Conference of State Legislatures, "For-Profit Colleges and Universities."

8. Seltzer, "Private Colleges and Universities."

9. Robinson, "Save our Public Universities."

Works Cited

Association of Governing Boards of Universities and Colleges (AGB).
  Consequential Board Governance in Public Higher Education Systems.
  Washington, DC: AGB, 2016. https://agb.org/sites/default/files
  /report_2016_public_governance.pdf.
——. *Effective Governing Boards: A Guide for Members of Governing Boards*
  of Independent Colleges and Universities. Washington, DC: AGB, 2009.
——. "Higher Education Must Change." *AGB Reports.* Washington, DC:
  AGB, May/June 1992.
——. *Policies, Practices, and Composition of Governing and Foundation*
  Boards 2016. Washington, DC: AGB, 2016.
Bennis, Warren, and Robert J. Thomas. "Crucibles of Leadership."
  Harvard Business Review, September 2002. https://hbr.org/2002/09
  /crucibles-of-leadership.
BoardMax. *The 2015 Board Engagement Report.* Cleveland, OH: BoardMax,
  2015, www.boardmax.com/2015-board-engagement-report/.
Bowen, William G. *The Board Book: An Insider's Guide for Directors and*
  Trustees. New York: W. W. Norton & Co., 2012.
Boyer, Ernest L. *Scholarship Reconsidered.* New York: Carnegie Foundation
  for Teaching, 1990.
Callan, Patrick, and Dean A. Honetschlager. *Policies for Improving Trustee*
  Selection in the Public Sector. Washington, DC: AGB, 1991.
Carlson, Scott. "When College Was a Public Good." *Chronicle of Higher*
  Education, November 27, 2016.
Carter, Jarrett. "Princeton Reaches $18M Settlement in Property Tax
  Case." *Education Dive,* October 18, 2016. https://www.educationdive
  .com/news/princeton-reaches-18m-settlement-in-property-tax-case
  /428498/.

——. "Survey: College Business Officers Say Higher Ed in Crisis." *Education Dive*, July 18, 2016. http://www.educationdive.com/news /survey-college-business-officers-say-higher-ed-in-crisis/422779/.

——. "What Makes a College President? Experts Weigh In on Critical Higher Ed Leadership Traits." *Education Dive*, October 17, 2016. http:// www.educationdive.com/news/what-makes-a-college-president/428149/.

——. "Why Turnover Is Growing in the College Presidency." *Education Dive*, July 18, 2016. http://www.educationdive.com/news/why-turn over-is-growing-in-the-college-presidency/422772/.

Chait, Richard. *Governance as Leadership: Reframing the Work of Nonprofit Boards*. Hoboken, NJ: John Wiley & Sons, 2005.

——. "The Gremlins of Governance." *Trusteeship*, August 2009. https:// agb.org/trusteeship/2009/julyaugust/the-gremlins-of-governance.

Chronicle of Higher Education. *Presidents and Board Chairs: Navigating the Future of Education Together*. Washington, DC: Chronicle of Higher Education, 2016. https://intoglobal.com/media/323748/2016 _PresidentsReport_Fall_v4_Into_Interactive.pdf.

City College of New York (CCNY). "About: Our History." https://www .ccny.cuny.edu/about/history.

City University of New York (CUNY). "Directory of U.S. Faculty Contracts and Bargaining Agents in Institutions of Higher Education." http://www.hunter.cuny.edu/ncscbhep.

Cole, Jonathan. *The Great American University*. New York: Public Affairs Press, 2009.

Deloitte Center for Board Effectiveness. "The Role of the Board in an Age of Exponential Change." March 2017. https://www2.deloitte.com/us /en/pages/center-for-the-edge/articles/board-in-age-of-exponential -change.html#.

Eliot, Charles W. *University Administration*. New York: Forgotten Books, 2015 (Boston and New York: Houghton-Mifflin, 1908).

"Evaluating the Board: The Next Dimension." *Chief Executive*, September 1995. https://www.thefreelibrary.com/Evaluating+the+board%3a +the+next+dimension.-a017536757.

Foley, Dennis. "To Fix Metro, Group Recommends Redoing WMATA." *WTOP*, November 26, 2016. http://wtop.com.

Greer, Darryl G. "Healthy Skepticism about Polls on College Value." American Association of State Colleges and Universities (AASCU)

Policy, November 11, 2016. https://medium.com/aascu-policy
/healthy-skepticism-about-polls-on-college-value-1b60ddb21c81.
——. *Prospective Governance*. Washington, DC: AGB, 1997.
Hampshire-Cowan, Artis. "The Four Cs of Board Leadership." *Trustee-
ship*, September/October 2016.
Harvard College. "Mission, Vision, and History." www.college.harvard
.edu/about/mission-and-vision.
Institute for College Access and Success. "Quick Facts about Student
Debt." March 2014. http://ticas.org/sites/default/files/legacy/files
/pub/Debt_Facts_and_Sources.
Institute of International Education. "Open Doors." https://www.iie
.org/opendoors.
Jaschik, Scott. "Admissions Group Calls for More Transparency on Use
of Agents to Recruit International Students." *Inside Higher Ed*,
September 26, 2016. https://www.insidehighered.com/news/2016/09
/26/admissions-group-calls-more-transparency-use-agents-recruit
-international-students.
——. "Pressure from All Sides: The 2015 Survey of Admissions
Directors." *Inside Higher Ed*, October 1, 2015. http://www.insidehighered
.com/print/news/survey/pressure-all-sides-2015-survey-admissions
-directors.
——. "Shocking Decision at Sweet Briar." *Inside Higher Ed*, March 4,
2015. http://www.insidehighered.com/news/2015/03/04/sweet-briar
-college-will-shut-down.
Jencks, Christopher, and David Riesman. *The Academic Revolution*. Garden
City, NJ: Doubleday, 1968.
June, Audrey Williams. "Adjuncts Build Strength in Numbers." *Chronicle
of Higher Education*, November 5, 2012. http://www.chronicle.com
/article/Adjuncts-Board-Strength-in/135520.
Kellerman, Barbara. "Leadership—It's a System, Not a Person." *Daedalus*
145, no. 3 (Summer 2016): 89–94.
Kerr, Clark, and Marian Gade. *The Guardians: Boards of Trustees of
American Colleges and Universities.* Washington, DC: Association of
Governing Boards of Universities and Colleges, 1989.
"Keys to Becoming a Successful Board Chair." *Board Forward*, April 2017.
http://www.boardforward.com/201704/Keys_to_Becoming_a
_Successful_Board_Chair.

Kirkpatrick, John E. *The Rise of Non-Resident Government in Harvard University and How Harvard Is Governed*. Ann Arbor, MI: G. Wehr, 1925.

Lederman, Doug. "Number of College Faculty and Staff Flattens." *Inside Higher Ed*, September 26, 2012.

———. "Number of Colleges and Universities Drops Sharply Amid Economic Turmoil." *Inside Higher Ed*, July 19, 2017. https://www.inside highered.com/news/2017/07/19/number-colleges-and-universities-drops -sharply-amid-economic-turmoil.

Legon, Richard. "The 10 Habits of Highly Effective Boards." *Trusteeship*, March/April 2014. http://agb.org/trusteeship/2014/3/10-habits-highly -effective-boards.

Leuty, Ron. "The Biggest Biotech You've Never Heard Of." *San Francisco Business Times*, August 30, 2013.

Lumina Foundation. *Strategic Plan for 2017 to 2025*. Indianapolis, IN: Lumina Foundation, 2016.

Machiavelli, Niccolò. *The Prince*, edited and translated by Robert M. Adams. New York: Norton, 1992.

Middle States Commission on Higher Education. *Standards for Accreditation and Requirements of Affiliation*. 13th ed. Philadelphia: Middle States Commission on Higher Education, 2014. http://www.msche.org /documents/RevisedStandardsFINAL.pdf.

Mitchell, Brian C. "The New Rules of Engagement." AAUP, June 6, 2013. https://www.aaup.org/taxonomy/term/1672/all.

———. "Suffolk University and the Collapse of Shared Governance." *Huffpost*, February 8, 2016. http://edvancefoundation.org/who-we-are/blog/.

National Association of Independent Colleges and Universities (NAICU). "College Board Releases 2016 Edition of Trends in College Pricing & Student Aid." Press release. October 26, 2016.

National Center for Education Statistics (NCES). "Digest of Educational Statistics." https://nces.ed.gov/programs/digest/.

———. "Fast Facts." https://nces.ed.gov/fastfacts/.

National Conference of State Legislatures. "For-Profit Colleges and Universities." September 23, 2013. http://www.ncsl.org/research /education/for-profit-colleges-and-universities.aspx.

Oliff, Phil, Vincent Palacios, Ingrid Johnson, and Michael Leachman. "Recent Deep State Higher Education Cuts May Harm Students and the Economy for Years to Come." Center on Budget and Policy Priorities,

March 19, 2013. http://www.cbpp.org/research/recent-deep-state
-higher-education-cuts-may-harm-students-and-the-economy-for
-years-to-come.

Redden, Elizabeth. "Number of International Branch Campuses Hits 250."
Inside Higher Ed, October 18, 2016. https://www.insidehighered.com.
/quicktakes/2016/10/18/number-international-branch-campuses-hits-250.

Reingold, Jennifer. "Theranos' Board: Plenty of Political Connections,
Little Relevant Expertise." *Fortune*, October 15, 2015. http://fortune.com
/2015/10/15/theranos-board-leadership.

Riddell, Roger. "Data Shows Decade's Dramatic Shift in Profile of
'Typical' College Student." *Education Dive*, July 11, 2017. http://www
.educationdive.com/news/data-shows-decades-dramatic-shift-in
-profile-of-typical-college-student/446723/.

Robinson, Marilynne. "Save Our Public Universities: In Defense of
America's Best Idea." *Harper's Magazine*, March 2016.

Schrecker, Ellen. "The Bad Old Days: How Higher Education Fared
during the Great Depression." *Chronicle Review*, June 16, 2009.

Scott, Robert. "The Modern American University: Observations from the
Field." *Oxford Magazine*, no. 365 (Fall 2015): 5-10.

———. "Revealing the Truth about Student Loan Debt." *Times Newsweekly*,
November 17, 2016.

Selingo, Jeffrey J. "The Job Nobody Can Seem to Keep: College President." *Washington Post*, July 15, 2016.

Selingo, Jeffrey J., Sonny Chheng, and Cole Clark. "Pathways to the
University Presidency: The Future of Higher Education Leadership."
Deloitte University Press, April 18, 2017. https://dupress.deloitte.com
/content/dam/dup-us-en/articles/3861_Pathways-to-the-university
-presidency/DUP_Pathways-to-the-university-presidency.pdf.

Seltzer, Rick. "Private Colleges and Universities Increase Tuition
Discounting Again in 2016-17." *Inside Higher Ed*, May 15, 2017.
https://www.insidehighered.com/news/2017/05/15/private-colleges
-and-universities-increase-tuition-discounting-again-2016-17.

———. "Small College Problems." *Inside Higher Ed*, September 23, 2016.
https://www.insidehighered.com/news/2016/09/23/small-colleges
-face-hurdles-theyre-pushed-change.

Sonnenfeld, Jeffrey A. "What Makes Great Boards Great." *Harvard
Business Review*, September 2002.

Stross, Randall. "Don't Blame Silicon Valley for Theranos." *New York Times*, April 27, 2016: A23.

"Sweezy v. New Hampshire." *Law and Higher Education*. http://www
.lawhigheredu.com/124-sweezy-v-new-hampshire.html#The_Supreme
_Court%E2%80%99s_Ruling.

Texas Public Policy Foundation, "'7 Solutions' Summary." http://www
.fgcu.edu/FacultySenate/files/11-4-2011_ATTACH_TX_7_Solutions
_Summary-1_copy.pdf.

Veblen, Thorstein. *The Higher Learning in America: A Memorandum on the
Conduct of Universities by Business Men*. Annotated edition edited and
with an introduction and notes by Richard F. Teichgraeber III.
Baltimore: Johns Hopkins University Press, 2015.

Wellesley College."Wellesley's Mission." www.wellesley.edu/about
/missionandvalues.

Suggestions for Further Reading

Adams, William W. "What the CEO Should Expect from the Board."
  Director's Monthly, vol. 20, no. 7 (July 1996).

Altbach, Philip G., Robert O. Berdahl, and Patricia J. Gumport. *Higher
  Learning in American Society.* Amherst, NY: Prometheus Books,
  1984.

American Association of University Professors (AAUP). "Statement on
  Government of Colleges and Universities." https://www.aaup.org
  /report/statement-government-colleges-and-universities.

"An Emerging Dimension of Strategy." *The EvoLLLution*, October 19, 2016.
  https://evolllution.com/.

Appleton, James R., and Stuart Dorsey. "The Chancellor's Role in a
  Presidential Transition." *Presidency*, vol. 12, no. 1 (2009): 30–32.

Areen, Judith. *Areen's Higher Education and the Law, Cases and Materials.*
  St. Paul, MN: West Academic, 2009.

Argyris, Chris, and Richard M. Cyert, *Leadership in the '80s: Essays on
  Higher Education.* Cambridge, MA: Institute for Educational Management, 1980.

Arnett, Autumn A. "Higher Ed Business Model Is Being Upended by Lack
  of Funding." *Inside Higher Ed*, October 25, 2016.

Ashby, Eric. "The Structure of Higher Education: A World View." *Higher
  Education,* vol. 2, no. 2 (May 73): 142–151.

Ashwell, Mark. "Take Responsibility for Ensuring Ethical Recruitment." *University World News*, September 30, 2016.

Asinov, Nanette. "UC: Millions Lost in Research Costs from Grants."
  SFGATE, June 16, 2010. http://www.sfgate.com/education/article/UC
  -Millions-lost-in-research-costs-from-grants-3185121.php.

Association of Governing Boards of Universities and Colleges (AGB).
    Board Assessment. Washington, DC: AGB. www.agb.org/consulting
    /services/board/assessment.

——. *Board Orientation*. Washington, DC: AGB. https://www.agb.org
    /briefs/board-orientation.

——. *Fiduciary Duties*. Washington, DC: AGB, 2015. https://www.agb
    .org/briefs/fiduciary-duties.

——. "Meeting the Leadership Challenge: Why the Most Effective
    Presidents and Chairs Seek Coaches." *Trusteeship*, March/April 2015.

——. *Statement on Board Responsibility for Institutional Governance*.
    Washington, DC: AGB, March 26, 2010.

——. *Top Public Policy Issues for Higher Education: 2017-2018*. Washington
    DC: AGB, 2017.

Atwell, Robert H. "The Craft of Presidential Assessment." *Trusteeship*,
    March/April 2007.

Bailar, Benjamin F. "Not-For-Profit Boards: Where Professionals Become
    Amateurs." *Director's Monthly*, vol. 21, no. 8 (August 1997).

Bakke, Dennis. *The Decision Maker*. Seattle, WA: Pear Press, 2013.

Berelson, Bernard. *Graduate Education in the United States*. New York:
    McGraw-Hill, 1960.

Berg, Maggie and Barbara K. Seeber. "Take Your Time: The Corporate
    University Steals It—Let's Grab It Back." *Chronicle of Higher Education*,
    July 3, 2016.

Biemiller, Lawrence. "Sweet Briar's Demise Puts New Pressure on
    College Trustees." *Chronicle of Higher Education*, May 4, 2015.

Blumenstyk, Goldie. "How For-Profit Education Is Now Embedded in
    Traditional Colleges." *Chronicle of Higher Education*, October 2016.

Bok, Derek. "Academic Values and the Lure of Profit." *Chronicle of Higher
    Education*, April 4, 2003.

——. *Higher Education in America*. Princeton, NJ: Princeton University
    Press, 2015.

——. *Higher Learning*. Cambridge, MA: Harvard University Press,
    1986.

——. "The Trouble with Shared Governance." *Trusteeship*, September/
    October 2013.

——. *Universities and the Future of America*. Durham, NC: Duke Univer-
    sity Press, 1990.

Bowen, William G.. *Inside the Boardroom: Governance by Directors and Trustees.* New York: John Wiley & Sons, 1994.

———. *Lessons Learned: Reflections of a University President.* Princeton, NJ: Princeton University Press, 2011.

Bowen, William G., and Eugene Tobin. *Locus of Authority: The Evolution of Faculty Roles in the Governance of Higher Education.* Princeton, NJ: Princeton University Press and ITHAKA, 2015.

Brown, Sarah. "Where the College Scorecard Has Gained Traction So Far—and Where It Hasn't." *Chronicle of Higher Education,* September 28, 2016.

Bruni, Frank. "The Lie about College Diversity." *New York Times,* December 13, 2015.

Burns, James MacGregor. *Leadership.* New York: HarperCollins, 2010.

Cabranes, Jose. "Myth and Reality of University Trusteeship in the Post-Enron Era." *76 Fordham Law Review,* rev. 955 (2007), http://ir .lawnet.fordham.edu/flr/vol76/iss2/15.

Cadbury, Sir Adrian. "Chairing the Board." *Director's Monthly,* vol. 21, no. 2 (February 1997).

———. *The Company Chairman.* Cambridge: Director Books published in association with the Institute of Directors, 1990.

Carter, Jarrett. "7 Frightening Trends in Higher Education." *Education Dive,* October 27, 2016.

———. "Current, Former Presidents Talk Higher Ed Disruption." *Education Dive,* October 21, 2016

———. "Experts Share Best Practices for Campus Scandal Rebound." *Education Dive,* December 13, 2016.

———. "Higher Ed Leaders Say Industry Is in Trouble." *Inside Higher Ed,* September 14, 2016.

———. "In Higher Ed Leadership Turnover, Data Show It's All about the Money." *Education Dive,* November 11, 2016.

———. "Manufacturing's Return Creates Greater Need from Higher Ed." *Education Dive,* June 9, 2016. http://www.educationdive.com/news /manufacturings-return-creates-greater-need-from-higher-ed/420598/.

———. "Small Colleges Facing Biggest Challenges with Enrollment." *Education Dive,* June 17, 2016.

———. "UL Board Ouster Could Be Subject to Supreme Court Approval." *Education Dive,* November 23, 2016.

———. "Why College Presidents Are Serving Much Shorter Terms." *Education Dive*, October 31, 2016.

Chait, Richard P., Thomas P. Holland, and Barbara E. Taylor, *Improving the Performance of Governing Boards.* Washington, DC: Rowman and Littlefield, 1996.

Chakrabarti, Rajashri, Michael Lovenheim, and Kevin Morris. "The Changing Higher Education Landscape: The Higher Education Market and Student Debt." *Liberty Street Economics*, September 6, 2016. http://libertystreeteconomics.newyorkfed.org/2016/09/the -changing-higher-education-landscape.html

"Changing How We Think about the Goals of Higher Education." *Tomorrow's Professor* (e-newsletter 1420), Stanford Center for Teaching and Learning. http://cgi.stanford.edu/~dept-ctl/cgi-bin /tomprof/enewsletter.php?msgno=1420.

Charan, Ram. *Boards That Deliver: Advancing Corporate Governance from Compliance to Competitive Advantage.* New York: John Wiley & Sons, 2005.

Chronicle of Higher Education. *The Past and Future of Higher Education.* Washington, DC: Chronicle of Higher Education, November 03, 2016.

———. *Reinventing the Academic Enterprise: College Leaders Consider the Challenges of the New Era.* Washington, DC: Chronicle of Higher Education, 2016.

Ciulla, Joanne B., ed. *Ethics, the Heart of Leadership.* Westport, CT: Praeger, 1998.

Cleveland, Harlan. *Nobody in Charge: Essays on the Future of Leadership.* San Francisco: Jossey-Bass, 2001.

———. *Seven Everyday Collisions in American Higher Education.* New York: International Council for Educational Development, 1974.

Coleman, Mary Sue. "After Years of Neglect, Public Higher Education Is at a Tipping Point." *Washington Post*, October 7, 2016.

College of New Rochelle. "Thanksgiving Comes Early for the College of New Rochelle." Statement. November 23, 2016.

"Creative Destruction." *Economist*, June 28, 2016.

Delbanco, Andrew. *College: What It Was, Is, and Should Be.* Princeton, NJ: Princeton University Press, 2012.

———. "Colleges: An Endangered Species?" *New York Review of Books*, March 10, 2005.

———. "The Endangered University." *New York Review of Books*, March 24, 2005.

Dew, John. "Global, Mobile, Vertical, and Social: The College Campus of Tomorrow." *The Futurist*, March-April 2010. https://www.questia.com /magazine/1G1-220203551/global-mobile-virtual-and-social-the-college -campus.

"Directory of U.S. Faculty Contracts and Bargaining Agents in Institutions of Higher Education." City University of New York. http://www .hunter.cuny.edu/ncscbhep.

Eckel, Peter, and Cathy Trower. "Boards Need to Be More Curious to Be Effective." *Inside Higher Ed*, May 15, 2017.

Education Advisory Board. *Reclaiming the Value of the Liberal Arts for the 21st Century*. Washington, DC: Education Advisory Board, 2016.

Ehrenberg, Ronald G. *Governing Academia*. Ithaca, NY: Cornell University Press, 2004.

"Engines of Growth." *Journal of the New England Board of Higher Education*, vol. 19, no. 4 (Winter 2005). http://www.nebhe.org/info/journal /issues/Connection_Winter05.pdf.

Epstein, Leon O. *Governing the University: The Campus and the Public Interest*. New York: John Wiley, 1974.

Fain, Paul. "Parents More Optimistic About Paying for College." *Inside Higher Ed*, September 28, 2016.

Farish, Donald J. "The Specific Threats Now Facing Higher Education." *Chronicle of Higher Education*, November 15, 2016.

Farrington, Dennis, and David Palfreyman. *The Law of Higher Education*. Oxford: Oxford University Press, 2012.

"Fiduciary Behavior: What's the Responsible Trustee to Do (and Not Do)?" *Trusteeship*, March/April 2013.

Fisher, James L. *The Board and the President*. New York: American Council on Education and Macmillan Publishing Company, 1991.

Fisher, James L., and Martha W. Tack, eds. *Leaders on Leadership: The College Presidency*. San Francisco: Jossey-Bass, 1988.

Flaherty, Colleen. "Survey of Presidents and Board Members Suggest Shared Governance Matters to Them but Could Be Improved Upon." *Inside Higher Ed*, September 29, 2016.

Flaherty, Colleen. "Writers Group Seeks Middle Ground on Campus Speech." *Inside Higher Ed*, October 18, 2016.

Gandossy, Robert, and Jeffrey Sonnenfeld, eds. *Leadership and Governance from the Inside Out.* Hoboken, NJ: John Wiley & Sons, 2004.

Garcia Mathewson, Tara. "Ed Dept Weighing Aid Options for Alternative Credentialing." *Education Dive*, July 22, 2015.

Gayle, Dennis John, Bhoendradatt Tewarie, and A. Quinton White, Jr. *Governance in the Twenty-First-Century University: Approaches to Effective Leadership and Strategic Management.* Hoboken, NJ: Wiley Periodicals, 2003.

Gerber, Larry. *The Rise and Decline of Faculty Governance: Professionalization and the Modern American University.* Baltimore: Johns Hopkins University Press, 2014.

Gladieux, Lawrence E. *Congress and the Colleges: National Politics and Higher Education.* Washington, DC: Lexington Books, 1976.

"Governance as Leadership: An Interview with Richard P. Chait." *Great Boards*, vol. 5, no. 2 (Summer 2005).

Grant, Gerald, and David Riesman. *The Perpetual Dream: Reform and Experiment in the American College.* Chicago: University of Chicago Press, 1978.

GrantThornton. "The State of Higher Education in 2017." *GrantThornton*, February 28, 2017. www.grantthornton.com/highered2017.

Greenblatt, Alan. "Why Being a University President Isn't a Stable Job Anymore." *Governing*, December 2016. http://www.governing.com/topics/education/gov-university-presidents-resign.html.

Hacker, Andrew. "The Truth about the Colleges." *New York Review of Books*, vol. 52, no. 17 (2005). http://www.nybooks.com/articles/2005/11/03/the-truth-about-the-colleges/.

Hamilton, Reeve. "Who's Behind the Proposed Reforms to Texas Higher Ed?" *Texas Tribune*, March 16, 2011.

Harvard Graduate School of Education. "Harvard Seminar for New Presidents." http://www.gse.harvard.edu/program/harvard-seminar-new-presidents.

Harvard University. *The Nature and Purposes of the University: A Discussion Memorandum. Interim Report.* Cambridge, MA: Harvard University, January 1971.

Havergal, Chris. "Public Higher Education 'Dying in the US,' Warns Robert Reich." *The World Academic Summit*, September 27, 2016.

Heilbron, Louis H. *The College and University Trustee: A View from the Board Room*. San Francisco: Jossey-Bass, 1973.

Heller, Donald E. "Why the U.S. Isn't Likely to Meet Obama's Goal on College Graduation Rates." *Hechinger Report*, October 2, 2014.

Herbst, Jurgen. *From Crisis to Crisis: American College Government, 1636–1819*. Cambridge, MA: Harvard University Press, 1982.

Hesselbein, Frances, Marshal Goldsmith, and Richard Beckhard, eds. *The Leader of the Future*. San Francisco: Jossey-Bass, 1996.

Hofstader, Richard. *The Development of Academic Freedom in the United States*. New York: Columbia University Press, 1955.

Hoover, Eric, and Sara Lipka. "Enrollment Goals Remain Elusive for Small Colleges." *Chronicle of Higher Education*, December 11, 2016.

Hundrieser, James. "The Impetus to Transform: Private Colleges Need to Develop New Business Model." *The EvoLLLution*, July 18, 2016.

Ingram, Richard T. *Governing Public Colleges and Universities: A Handbook for Trustees, Chief Executives, and Other Campus Leaders*. San Francisco: Jossey-Bass in joint publication with the AGB, 1993.

———. "A Test of an Effective Board." *Trusteeship*, May/June 2003.

Jackson, Robert. "A Corporate Governance Gadfly." Harvard Law School Corporate Governance Blog, April 19, 2007. https://corpgov.law.harvard.edu/2007/04/19/a-corporate-gadfly/.

Jaschik, Scott. "Author Discusses New Book about How American Higher Education Has Always Been 'A Perfect Mess.'" *Inside Higher Ed*, May 3, 2017.

———. "Many Students Opt for Colleges That Spend More on Nonacademic Functions, Study Finds." *Inside Higher Ed*, January 29, 2013.

———. "New Version of Proposal to Regulate Endowments." *Inside Higher Ed*, December 7, 2016.

———. "Suffolk President, Facing Dismissal, Quits." *Inside Higher Ed*, July 29, 2016.

Johnson, Sandra S., and Peter Eckel. *The Last 100 Days of a Presidency: What Boards Need to Know and Do*. Washington, DC: AGB, May/June 2013.

Kail, Col. Eric. "Leadership Character: The Role of Empathy." *Washington Post*, October 28, 2011.

Kamarck, Elaine C. *Why Presidents Fail And How They Can Succeed Again*. Washington, DC: Brookings Institution Press, 2016.

Kaplan, Gabriel E. "Do Governance Structures Matter?" *New Directions for Higher Education*, vol. 127 (Fall 2004).

Kaplin, William A. *The Law of Higher Education 1980.* San Francisco: Jossey-Bass, 1980.

Kaplin, William A., and Barbara A. Lee. *The Law and Higher Education.* San Francisco: Jossey-Bass, 2007.

Kaufman, Clare. "The History of Higher Education in the United States." *WorldWideLearn.* http://www.worldwidelearn.com/education-advisor /indepth/history-higher-education.php.

"Keeping an Effective Not-For-Profit Board." *GrantThornton*, 2016. https://www.slideshare.net/GrantThorntonUS/keeping-an-effective -notforprofit-board.

Keller, Morton, and Phyllis Keller. *Making Harvard Modern: The Rise of America's University.* New York: Oxford University Press, 2001.

Kellerman, Barbara. *Bad Leadership: What It Is, How It Happens, Why It Matters?* Boston: Harvard Business Publishing, 2004.

Keohane, Nannerl O. *Thinking about Leadership.* Princeton, NJ: Princeton University Press, 2012.

Kezar, Adrianna, and Daniel Maxey, eds. *Envisioning the Faculty for the 21st Century: Moving to a Mission-Oriented and Learner-Centered Model.* New Brunswick, NJ: Rutgers University Press, 2016.

Kezar, Adrianna, and Elizabeth Holcombe. "The Professoriate Reconsidered." *Academe*, November-December 2015. https://www.aaup.org /article/professoriate-reconsidered#.WSCa5bvyve0.

Khurana, Rakesh. *Handbook of Leadership Theory and Practice.* Boston: Harvard Business Press, 2013.

Kiley, Kevin. "Reign of the Politician-Chancellor." *Inside Higher Ed*, August 23, 2011.

Kirkpatrick, John E. *Academic Organization and Control.* Yellow Springs, OH: Antioch Press, 1931.

Kirp, David L. "Conquering the Freshman Fear of Failure." *New York Times*, August 20, 2016.

Kohler, Jurgen. "Impacts of Transparency on Governance and Accountability." Meeting of the Directors General for Higher Education, September 2010. http://media.ehea.info/file/Transparency_Namur _September_2010/92/3/Impacts_of_Transparency_on_Governance _and_accountability_599923.pdf.

Kovacs, Kasia. "2016 Ballot Measures That Have an Impact on Higher Education." *Inside Higher Ed*, November 2, 2016.

Kravjar, Julius, and Marek Hladik. "The Ethical Hole at the Centre of 'Publish or Perish.'" *University World News*, September 30, 2016.

Kreighbaum, Andrew. "Judge Grants Injunction Blocking Governor's Replacement of the U of Louisville Board." *Inside Higher Ed*, August 1, 2016.

Lane, Jason E., and D. Bruce Johnstone. *Higher Education Systems 3.0: Harnessing Systemness, Delivering Performance*. Albany, NY: SUNY Press, 2013.

"Langone on Leadership." *Leaders Magazine, Inc.* vol. 37, no. 4 (2014). http://www.leadersmag.com/issues/2014.4_Oct/PDFs/LEADERS -Kenneth-Langone-Invemed-Associates.pdf.

Leavitt, Harold J., and Thomas L. Whisler. "Managing Higher Education in the 80s: Trying to Do More with Less." *Harvard Business Review*, November 1958.

Lederman, Doug. "Culling of Higher Ed Begins." *Inside Higher Ed*, July 19, 2017.

———. "Southern Accreditor Places 10 on Probation, Including Louisville and New UT Campus." *Inside Higher Ed*, December 7, 2016.

Lee, Thomas. "Federal Criminal Probe of Theranos Rings Hollow." *San Francisco Chronicle*, May 11, 2016.

Livermore, Rufus. *Livermore's Trustees Handbook: A Manual for the Use of Trustees, Executors, Administrators, Assigne*. New York: L.K. Strouse & Co., 1885.

Lombardi, John V. *How Universities Work*. Baltimore: Johns Hopkins University Press, 2013.

Lucas, Sara Ivey. "Trusteeship." *Learning to Give*. https://www.learningto give.org/resources/trusteeship.

Ma, Jennifer, Sandy Baum, Matea Pender, and Meredith Welch. *Trends in College Pricing 2016*. New York: College Board, 2016. https://trends .collegeboard.org/sites/default/files/2016-trends-college-pricing-web_1.pdf

Marcus, Jon. "Once Invisible, College Boards of Trustees Are Suddenly in the Spotlight." *The Hechinger Report*, April 30, 2015.

Martin, James, James E. Samuels, and associates. *Presidential Transitions in Higher Education: Managing Leadership Change*. Baltimore: Johns Hopkins University Press, 2004.

Matthews, George J., Norman R. Smith, and Bryan E. Carlson. *What College Trustees Need to Know*. Bloomington, IN: iUniverse, 2013.

McClure, Charles. "Review of *A Test of Leadership: Charting the Future of U.S. Higher Education*, by Commission Appointed by Secretary of Education Margaret Spellings." *The Library Quarterly: Information, Community, Policy* vol. 77, no. 1 (pre-publication copy, September 2006): 89–92. doi: 10.1086/512957.

Miller, Timothy M. "Exploring University Presidents' Decision-Making Processes throughout Their Tenure in Office." PhD diss., George Washington University, May 2016.

Millstein, Ira M. "How Corporate America Can Survive These Uncertain Times." *Fortune*, January 26, 2017. http://fortune.com/2017/01/26/donald-trump-economic-uncertainty/.

Mitchell, Brian C. "Consolidation in Higher Education: The Clash between Data and Optics." Edvance Foundation, September 18, 2016. http://edvancefoundation.org/blog/consolidation-in-higher-education-the-clash-between-data-and-optics/.

———. "Grading Higher Education: When Worlds Collide." Edvance Foundation, October 25, 2016. http://edvancefoundation.org/blog/grading-higher-education-when-worlds-collide/.

———. "When the Going Gets Tough for Public Universities: Go Private?" Edvance Foundation, December 5, 2016. http://edvancefoundation.org/blog/when-the-going-gets-tough-for-public-universities-go-private/.

———. "When a Major Employer Closes: Local Lessons from St. Joseph's College." Edvance Foundation, February 13, 2017. http://edvancefoundation.org/blog/when-a-major-employer-closes-local-lessons-from-st-josephs-college/.

Morison, Samuel Eliot. *The Founding of Harvard College*. Cambridge, Massachusetts: Harvard University Press, 1938.

———. *Harvard College in the Seventeenth Century*. Cambridge, MA: Harvard University Press, 1936.

———. *Precedence at Harvard in the Seventeenth Century*. Worcester, MA: The Davis Press, 1932.

———. *Three Centuries of Harvard, 1636–1936*. Cambridge, MA: Harvard University Press, 1936.

Morison, Samuel Eliot et al. *The History and Traditions of Harvard College*. Cambridge, MA: Harvard Crimson, 1934.

Mukunda, Gautam. *Indispensible: When Leaders Really Matter.* Boston: Harvard Business Review Press, 2012.

Munitz, Barry. "Higher Education Must Change." *AGB Reports*, May/June 1992, 17.

Nadler, David A. "Building Better Boards." *Harvard Business Review*, May 2004. https://hbr.org/2004/05/building-better-boards.

Natale, Samuel M., John B. Wilson, and Linda S. Perry. *The Moral Manager.* Binghamton, NY: Global Publications, Binghamton University, 2002.

National Association of Corporate Directors (NACD). *Report of the NACD Blue Ribbon Commission on Performance Evaluation of Chief Executive Officers, Boards, and Directors.* Washington DC: National Association of Corporate Directors, 1994.

National Center for Education Statistics (NCES). *Completing College: A National View of Student Attainment Rates.* NCES Signature Report 4, November 12, 2012. https://nces.ed.gov/programs/coe/indicator_csa.asp.

New, Jake. "Academic Fraud at California State Northridge." *Inside Higher Ed*, December 8, 2016.

———. "College Police Say Recent Incidents Serve as Reminder of Dangers of the Job." *Inside Higher Ed*, December 2, 2016.

———. "Despite Long Odds, Universities Start or Resume Big-Time Football Programs." *Inside Higher Ed*, July 18, 2016.

Newfield, Christopher. *The Great Mistake: How We Wrecked Public Universities and How We Can Fix Them.* Baltimore: Johns Hopkins University Press, 2016.

New Jersey Association of State Colleges and Universities. *College Affordability Study Commission.* Trenton, New Jersey: New Jersey Association of State Colleges and Universities, 2016.

Newman, Frank, and Lara Couturier and Jamie Scurry. *The Future of Higher Education: Rhetoric, Reality and the Risks of the Market.* San Francisco: Jossey-Bass, 2004.

O'Byrne, Darren, and Christopher Bond. "Back to the Future: The Idea of a University Revisited." *Journal of Higher Education Policy and Management*, vol. 36, no. 6 (2014): 571-584.

Organization for Economic Co-operation and Development (OECD). *G20/OECD Principles of Corporate Governance: OECD Report to G20*

Finance Ministers and Central Bank Governors. Paris: OECD, September 2015.

Palfreyman, David, ed. *The Oxford Tutorial.* Oxford: OxCHEPS, 2008.

Palmer, Iris, Kim Dancy, and Ben Barrett. "Past Is Prologue: State and Local Funding for Higher Education in the Next Recession." *New America,* November 2016.

PEN America. *And Campus for All: Diversity, Inclusion, and Free Speech at U.S. Universities.* New York: PEN America: October, 2016.

PennAHEAD. *Academic Freedom, Tenure, and Shared Governance. What's AHEAD,* University of Pennsylvania, 2016. https://www.ahead-penn.org/sites/default/files/u2/PA_WA_Poll11_Report_WEB.pdf.

Perkins, James A. *Reform of Higher Education: Mission Impossible?* New York: International Council for Educational Development, 1971.

Pierce, Susan Resnick. *Governance Reconsidered: How Boards, Presidents, Administrators, and Faculty Can Help Their Colleges Thrive.* San Francisco: Jossey-Bass, 2014.

Price, Terry L. *Understanding Ethical Failures in Leadership.* Cambridge, UK: Cambridge University Press, 2006.

PricewaterhouseCooper, LLC. *Perspectives in Higher Education 2014.* 2014. https://www.pwc.co.za/en/assets/pdf/perspectives-in-higher-education-2014.pdf.

Rawlings, Hunter. "College Is Not a Commodity. Stop Treating It Like One." *Washington Post,* June 9, 2016.

Redden, Elizabeth. "Conditional Admission and Pathway Programs Proliferate." *Inside Higher Ed,* January 3, 2013.

Registry for College and University Presidents. http://www.registryinterim.com/.

Reiter, Noah. "Initial Lesson from OSU Tragedy." *RaveMobileSafety,* December 1, 2016.

Rhodes, Frank H. T. *The Creation of the Future: The Role of the American University.* Ithaca, NY: Cornell University Press, 2001.

Riesman, David. *Constraints and Variety in American Education.* Garden City, NY: Doubleday, 1958.

———. *On Higher Education.* San Francisco: Jossey-Bass, 1980.

Rollert, John Paul. "What Adam Smith Can Teach Us About Incentives in Higher Education." *Boston Review,* November 04, 2013.

Rosovsky, Henry. *The University: An Owner's Manual.* New York: W. W. Norton, 1990.

Rothman, Joshua. "Shut Up and Sit Down: Why the Leadership Industry Rules." *New Yorker,* February 29, 2016.

Rudolf, Frederick. *The American College and University: A History.* New York: Random House, 1962.

Ruff, Corinne. "Many Colleges Profited From Slavery: What Can They Do About It Now?" *Chronicle of Higher Education,* April 16, 2016.

SallieMae. "How America Saves for College 2016." https://www.salliemae .com/plan-for-college/how-america-saves-for-college.

Samet, Elizabeth, ed. *Leadership: Essential Writings by Our Greatest Thinkers: A Norton Anthology.* New York: W. W. Norton, 2015.

Schmidt, Peter. "Why University Chiefs Head Out the Door." *Chronicle of Higher Education,* November 10, 2016.

Schuessler, Jennifer. "Yale Sets Policy That Could Allow Renaming of Calhoun College." *New York Times,* December 2, 2016.

Schwartz, Merrill Pellows. *A National Survey of Presidential Performance Assessment Policies and Practices.* Washington DC: AGB, 1998.

Scott, Robert A. "Assuring Effectiveness and Productivity in Higher Education." *On Course* [newsletter]. New York: Grant Thornton, October 2011.

———. "College Student Loans: Lifting the Veil on the Truth." *Queens (NY) Courier,* November 27, 2016.

———. "Community Development, University Style." *Garden City News,* May 17, 2013.

———. "The Curriculum as Covenant." *The College Board Review,* no. 121 (Fall 1981): 20–28.

———. "The Modern American University: A Love Story." *On the Horizon,* vol. 18, Issue 4 (Fall 2010).

———. "Thinking about Students: A Personal Perspective." *On the Horizon,* 25, no. 3 (2017).

Selingo, Jeffrey J. "As College Tuitions Rise, Scholarships Fail to Keep Pace." *LinkedIn,* September 20, 2016. https://www.linkedin.com/pulse /college-tuitions-rise-scholarships-fail-keep-pace-jeff-selingo.

Seltzer, Rick. "Interest Rises in Politicians as University Presidents." *Inside Higher Ed,* October 7, 2016.

———. "Judge Blocks Kentucky Governor from Overhauling Louisville Board." *Inside Higher Ed*, September 29, 2016.

———. "Moody's Sees Stable Outlook for Higher Ed in 2017." *Inside Higher Ed*, December 7, 2016.

———. "Panelists Warn of International Student Bubble." *Inside Higher Ed*, September 26, 2016. https://www.*Inside Higher Ed*.com/news/2016/09 /23/small-colleges-face-hurdles-theyre-pushed-change.

———. "Q&A with Author of Book on Universities' Intellectual Property Practices." *Inside Higher Ed*, December 5, 2016.

———. "Survey Finds Gender Gap in Presidential Spouse Expectations." *Inside Higher Ed*, January 10, 2017.

Sharma, Yojana. "Universities Must Think Outside the Box to Embrace Change." *University World News*, September 30, 2016.

Shattock, Michael, ed. *International Trends in University Governance: Autonomy, Self-Governance and the Distribution of Authority.* London: Routledge, 2014.

———, ed. *Managing Good Governance in Higher Education.* Maidenhead, Berkshire, London, UK: Open University Press, 2006

———. *Managing Successful Universities.* Maidenhead, Berkshire, London, UK: Open University Press, 2003.

———, ed. *The Structure & Governance of Higher Education.* Research into Higher Education Monographs. Surrey: Society for Research into Higher Education, 1983.

Smith, Wilson, and Thomas Bender, eds. *American Higher Education Transformed 1940-2005: Documenting the National Discourse.* Baltimore: Johns Hopkins University Press, 2008.

Soares, Louis, Patricia Steele, and Lindsay Wayt. *Evolving Higher Education Business Models: Leading with Data to Deliver Results.* Washington, DC: American Council on Higher Education, September 2015.

Sonnenfeld, Jeffrey A. "What Makes Great Boards Great." *Harvard Business Review*, September 2002.

Stein, Ronald H., and Stephen Joel Trachtenberg. *The Art of Hiring in America's Colleges and Universities.* Amherst, NY: Prometheus Books, 1993.

Stewart, James B. "How Much Graduates Earn Drives More College Rankings." *New York Times*, October 20, 2016.

Stripling, Jack. "A Higher-Ed Needler Finds Its Moment." *Chronicle of Higher Education*, April 10, 2016.

Temmerman, Nita. "Does Your Academic Board Work Properly?" *University World News*, August 12, 2016.

Thelin, John R. *A History of American Higher Education*. Baltimore: Johns Hopkins University Press, 2004.

Thornburgh, John K. "360 degree support, 24/7 President." *Trusteeship*, March/April 2007.

TIAA-CREF Institute. "Board Governance at a Crossroads." www.tiaa-crefinstitute.org.

Tierney, William G., ed. *Competing Conceptions of Academic Governance: Negotiating the Perfect Storm*. Baltimore: Johns Hopkins University Press, 2004.

Toner, Mark. *The Highly Endangered Business Model (and How to Fix It)*. Washington, DC: American Council on Education, Summer 2015.

Trachtenberg, Stephen Joel, Gerald B. Kauver, and E. Grady Bogue. *Presidencies Derailed: Why University Leaders Fail and How to Prevent It*. Baltimore: Johns Hopkins University Press, 2013.

Trammell, Jeffrey. "5 Steps for an Effective Board Chair (Excerpt)." AGB blog, July 19, 2016. https://www.agb.org/store/effective-board-chairs-a-guide-for-university-and-college-chairs.

———. *Effective Board Chairs: A Guide for University and College Chairs*. Washington, DC: AGB, 2016.

Trower, Cathy A. *Govern More, Manage Less: Harnessing the Power of Your Nonprofit Board*. Washington, DC: BoardSource, 2010.

———. *The Practitioner's Guide to Governance and Leadership: Building High-Performing Nonprofit Boards*. Hoboken, NJ: Jossey-Bass/Wiley, 2013.

Truman Commission on Higher Education. *Higher Education for Democracy: A Report of the President's Commission on Higher Education*. New York: Harper and Brothers, 1947.

Truskie, Stanley D. *CEO Performance Evaluation*. Pittsburgh, PA: Management and Science Development, 1995.

Tuchman, Barbara W. *The March of Folly: From Troy to Vietnam*. New York: Random House, 1985.

University of Oklahoma. *Regent's Policy Manual for the University of Oklahoma*. Norman, OK: University of Oklahoma. http://www.ou.edu/regents/official_agenda/CurrentPolicyManual.pdf.

Veysey, Laurence R. *The Emergence of the American University.* Chicago: University of Chicago Press, 1970.

Watanabe, Teresa. "Five Things to Know about What America's College Freshman Are Thinking." *LA Times*, May 1, 2017.

Widmayer, Charles E. *Hopkins of Dartmouth: The Story of Ernest Martin Hopkins and His Presidency of Dartmouth College.* Hanover, NH: Dartmouth College through the University Press of New England, 1977.

———. *John Sloan Dickey: A Chronicle of His Presidency of Dartmouth College.* Hanover, NH: Dartmouth College through the University Press of New England. 1991.

Wingspread Group on Higher Education. *An American Imperative: Higher Expectations for Higher Education: An Open Letter to Those Concerned about the American Future.* Racine, WI: Johnson Foundation, 1993.

Wolfe, Alan. "The Vanishing Big Thinker." *Chronicle Review*, July 28, 2016.

Woodhouse, Kellie. "Lazy Rivers and Student Debt." *Inside Higher Ed.* June 15, 2015.

Index